The Creative Self

Tracy Kline

Ars Omnia Press

Cover Art: Don Hazlitt

ISBN: 978-1477444474

Ars Omnia Press

Visit our website at:
www.arsomnia.org

This book is dedicated to Don Hazlitt and Damian Hey, who, as living embodiments of the creative spirit in action, have inspired countless students thoughout the years to realize their own creative potentials. This book would not have been possible without their inspiration.

CONTENTS

INTRODUCTION

If you are like most people, you probably never gave much thought to your own creative potential. Life for the vast majority of human beings living in the 21st century is so filled with conflicting obligations, endless commitments, social expectations, frenzied activity, and financial pressures that the idea of spending even a few moments each day tapping into your own creative energy probably seems like a fairly frivolous proposition. After all, with the myriad of pressing demands that are placed upon us each and every day, who the hell has the time to spend engaged in creative activities that don't seem to serve any practical purpose?

Besides, you may be thinking, all this talk about creativity may be fine and dandy for those relatively few individuals who work in artistic fields—writers, painters, filmmakers, and graphic designers perhaps—but it doesn't seem all that relevant to ordinary people trying to live out their everyday lives.

Think again. The ability to engage in creative self-expression, along with our ability to engage in higher order reasoning, is what separates human beings from all other animals. Most of the other things that we do in life—eat, procreate, sleep, make sense of our surroundings—can be done, to a greater or lesser extent by any other animal. But only a human being can philosophize about the nature of reality, and only a human being is able to express him or herself creatively. Chimpanzees may be able to use simple instruments, establish communities, and communicate with one another, but no chimp has ever painted a Sistine Chapel or built a gothic cathedral.

The point I'm trying to make here is that in some ways you are really not living a fully human life if all you do is eat, work, sleep, party, and watch football on T.V. If that is the full extent of your daily activities, you might as well be a baboon. I would argue that to be a fully flourishing human being it is necessary to engage in those pursuits that are uniquely human. And, as I have already indicated, creative self-expression is one of the most significant of these.

In the 21ˢᵗ century, it will also be more important than ever to have people who are able to think creatively about many of the seemingly overwhelming problems facing our planet. The simple paradigms of the past will not enable us to tackle huge problems like global warming, the unequal distribution of planetary resources, and the ever-present threat of terrorism. We need to have people around who are capable of thinking "outside the box" in new and bold ways if our species is going to survive beyond this century.

"But I'm Not The Creative Type!"

You might also be thinking that, even if it would be wonderful to become more creative in your daily life, you are not the creative type. Perhaps you've never picked up a paintbrush before or have never even given a passing thought to trying to write a poem or a play. Maybe you've spent much of your life working in fields that don't require any kind of creative input at all, so you question whether you have it in you to be a creative type.

The aim of this little book is to show you that, not only do you have the potential to become more creative in your everyday life, but that the true source of your own creative potential lies closer than you can possibly imagine. It lies

>   deep within the very marrow of your being
>   in the nooks and crannies that comprise
>   the essence of who you are as a human being...
>   in the lines that cross your craggy face,
>   in ordinary, silly, everyday relationships with others
>   in the volatile, erratic emotions that well up inside
>   each of us
>   in those rare moments of sublime perfection
>   accessible to all of us
>   but normally never fully realized.

To put it simply, you are your own magnificent work of art...better than anything that Michelangelo or Picasso could produce. The problem is that you just don't realize it.

And that's a terribly sad thing. Imagine, going through life with all that creative potential locked up inside of you, but never having the opportunity or the inclination to give it voice. It's rather like having the ability to soar through the air like a majestic eagle, but choosing instead to bury yourself underground like a frightened mole. Like all human beings, you have the latent potential to soar to dazzling heights of self-realization. All you need to do is have the courage to take the first bold leap.

That's where this book comes in. There have been many works written in recent years on creativity and creative theory, but this book is a bit different insofar as it places the emphasis on the process of self-discovery as a catalyst for creative exploration and discovery. You see, I have this wacky, unshakable belief that you—that's right, you!—are actually quite fascinating. Your life is filled with the stuff of novels, poems, paintings, and plays. In every silly, stupid, depressing, exhilarating event of your life, in every single thought that runs through the chatterbox of your chaotic mind, there is an amazing epic in the making.

What I would like to do is to help you start paying attention to your own life through a bit of much needed self-reflection, and to use whatever comes out of this experience as fodder for creative inspiration and activity. I guarantee that what you produce as a result of this process of self-discovery will be incredible because it is a reflection of who you are, and you, my dear friend, are utterly and completely incredible (whether you believe it or not).

This doesn't mean that I am promising that by the end of this book you will be writing poetry like Shakespeare or starting to paint like Rembrandt (the world probably doesn't need another Shakespeare or Rembrandt anyway). What I do promise is that, if you accept the basic premise that you have the potential for creative self-expression, you will create works of art that uniquely express who you are as a human being, and, in the process of doing so, you will discover much more about yourself than you ever could have otherwise.

And the best thing about what we are going to attempt to achieve as a result of our exercises is that there is no right or wrong, better or worse, way to proceed. So you can't ever screw up anytime you attempt to express yourself in writing, because simply by taking this first step you have already proceeded in traveling down the winding road of self-discovery. And that is really what this book is all about.

The Creative Self Program

The 15 week Creative Self Program begins with something that you are very, very familiar with—namely YOU. The goal of this program is to compel you to start looking at what is happening around you—and even more importantly inside you—as a jumping off point for creative self-discovery. Theoretically, there is nothing and no one that you know better than yourself, and there is nothing that is more intrinsically fascinating to you than your own life experiences.

If this sounds like a dubious proposition, just take a few moments to step back and observe the thoughts flowing through your own mind right now. If you watch the patter of your own thoughts for any period of time, it is probably true that—unless you have already attained enlightenment like the Buddha or Christ—the thoughts that you will observe are almost exclusively related to your own life experience (your own shit, in other words). Even the thoughts you may have about other people are probably inextricably linked to how you feel about these people, how they have treated you, or what they may be thinking about you.

For better or worse, most human beings are ego-driven creatures, who typically interpret reality in terms of their own needs, wants, desires, fears, and expectations. It is not within the scope of our discussion in this work to assess whether the self-absorption of most human beings is a good or bad thing or whether there is any realistic way to transcend our own auto-fixated approach to life (There are plenty of self-help books that address those issues). From the perspective of this program, human self-absorption is actually an interesting object of examination, a tool for deep self-discovery, and most importantly a potentially viable source of creative inspiration. In other words, we will use what religion, ethics, and pop psychology have always interpreted as a negative—human egocentrism—and see how it can be used for something positive, constructive, and uplifting.

Tools of the Trade

In the past the tools of creative expression were fairly simple and relatively inexpensive: a bit of canvas, some brushes and paints, a few pieces of paper, and some writing implements. These are still perfectly fine tools to use in order to begin the process of creative self-exploration. In the technological age in which we live, however, there are other tools that we can use to develop creative potential, and I would encourage you to explore as many of these as possible. :

You definitely want to have a pen (or pencil if you prefer) and paper available to jot down your ideas and creative inspirations. Some people keep scraps of paper all around their home and office so that when inspiration strikes them they can jot down ideas, develop future projects, or just doodle. Keeping a creativity notebook is even better, because it enables you to keep a continuous log of observations, ideas, fragments of new poems, and possible future projects. A small notebook that can easily fit into your pocket or purse is ideal because you can carry it with you on the go and write in it as needed.

Other people prefer to bypass the pen and paper experience and do their writing on the computer, either using a word processing program like Microsoft Word or blogging programs like Blogger (blogger.com) or Wordpress (wordpress.com). Writing creative pieces directly onto the computer certainly has its advantages: it's easy to revise what you've written and you don't have to worry about being able to read your own scrawl later on. Blogging programs go one step further, enabling you to share what you've written with the entire blogosphere and get feedback from folks who are interested in the creative process.

The process of creative self-expression, of course, doesn't have to focus solely on writing. Though that's the specific focus of this particular program, you should always feel free to follow your inspirations whereever they lead. That might mean leaving the pen and paper (or keyboard) for a while and working with a digital camera, a sketchpad, paint and canvas, video camera , or just about any other creative medium that you care to try. If you've ever been to a museum of contemporary art, you are undoubtedly aware that just about any material can be used in the creative act.

The Most Important Tool of All

Of course, the most important tool that you will need in order to fully explore your own creative potential is a primal sense of wanton wackiness. This is nothing more than the willingness to stretch yourself artistically beyond your own comfort zone, to risk the disapproval of sterile, conformist society by being determined to create something vibrant, captivating, and potentially unsettling, and to go where your own vital creative spirit leads you, regardless of the risks. If you have this sort of radical openness to exploration and experimentation, you don't need many other creative tools, and you will almost certainly create something fascinating in the process.

It also helps if you are willing to view the entire creative process as a kind of play. When you were a child, I'm sure that you looked forward to playtime. You didn't have to be too serious when you were playing and you didn't have to accomplish anything monumental. You played just for the fun of it. The creative process should be viewed in a similar way. You create in order to have a good time. If you're not enjoying yourself, you are definitely doing something wrong. So next time you start thinking about whether what you are producing is "good enough," try to revert back to the five-year-old you once were, stop criticizing yourself so damn much, relax, and start playing.

Good luck and good creating!

Creative Concepts

1

What Is Creativity Anyway?

Since this is a book about the creative self (whatever that is) it seems to make sense before we start our amazing voyage of self-exploration, to get a handle on what we mean by the words "creative" and "creativity." After all, we throw these words around all the time in everyday life, but it often seems as though we really don't have a very clear conception about what we mean when we use these terms. Americans have this crazy tendency to refer to so many things as "creative"soap operas, politicians, recipes, mechanics, electronic devices —that the word has almost lost any real meaning in our culture.

If you go to the dictionary and look up the word creativity, you will find an incredible variety of definitions. Even those who are supposed to be experts in the field of Creative Studies seem to have widely divergent ideas about what the term means. Just look at a handful of the many ways that creativity has been defined in recent years, and you will immediately see just what an elusive concept the term appears to be:

- "the ability to look at the same thing as everyone else but see something different." (Chic Thompson)
- "Definition of the creative act—the combination of previously unrelated structures in such a way that you get more out of the emergent whole than you have put in." (Arthur Koestler)
- "the process of bringing something new into being...creativity

requires passion and commitment. Out of the creative act is born symbols and myths. It brings to our awareness what was previously hidden and points to new life. The experience is one of heightened consciousness and ecstasy." (Rollo May)

- "creativity consists largely of rearranging what we know in order to find out what we do not know…Hence, to think creatively we must be able to look afresh at what we normally take for granted." (George Kneller)

- "the tendency to express and activate all the capacities of the organism to the extent that such activities enhance the organism or the self." (Carl Rogers)

- "One man may be discovering a way to relieve pain, whereas another is devising a new and more subtle form of torture for political prisoners. Both these actions seem to be creative, even though their social value is very different." (Eric Fromm)

- "Though my fantasies may be extremely novel, they cannot usefully be described as creative unless they eventuate in some useful product—unless they are symbolized in words, or written in a poem, or translated into a work of art, or fashioned into an invention." (Eric Fromm)

Examine these definitions closely enough and certain key characteristics of what we refer to as "creativity" seem to stand out. You may want to jot some of these common characteristics down to see if you can make some sense of these divergent ideas.

Exploring the Concept

As you can see, there is no universal definition of creativity that everyone can agree with. However, novelty, interplay, and utility seem to be somewhat essential to any truly creative act. Typically we describe someone as being creative if they devise something new (novelty) out of the combination of previously existing but unrelated elements (interplay), and in doing so produce something—an idea, a product, or a work of art—that others can use or enjoy (utility).

Novelty. The element of novelty in particular seems to be central to the idea of creativity. According to George Kneller, novelty "springs largely from the rearrangement of existing knowledge—a rearrangement that is itself an addition to knowledge. Such rearrangement reveals an unsuspected kinship between facts long known but wrongly believed to be strangers to one another." Kellner goes on to say that when I express an idea or form that is new to *me*—even if it is obvious to others—a certain amount of creativity may in fact be at work. But the highest level of creativity is one that "shatters the mold of custom and extends the possibility of thought and perception." This sort of creative enterprise can expand the boundaries of art and science for all human beings. (4)

   We witness such novelty every time a poet or writer combines words or images in new ways using metaphors. Take the following selection from Beat writer Allen Ginsberg's poem "America":

> America I've given you all and now I'm nothing.
> America two dollars and twentyseven cents January 17, 1965.
> I can't stand my own mind.
> America when will we end the human war?
> Go fuck yourself with your atom bomb.
> I don't feel good don't bother me.
> I won't write my poem till I'm in my right mind.
> America when will you be angelic?
> When will you take off your clothes?
> When will you look at yourself through the grave?
> When will you be worthy of your million Trotskyites?
> America why are your libraries full of tears?
> America when will you send your eggs to India?
> I'm sick of your insane demands.
> When can I go into the supermarket and buy what I need with my good looks?

In this poem Ginsberg is essentially writing a plea to the citizens of the United States to live up to the ideals upon which the country was founded. What makes his writing interesting, however, is the unexpected juxtaposition of certain ideas which at first glance seem to have nothing at all to do with the point of the poem—the poet's sick state, his love of nudity, the joke about the supermarket (Ginsberg would definitely not have been able to buy anything with his "good looks"). The poem works precisely because of these sorts of jarring, original elements.

   While novelty is essential to the creative act, it comes with a price. Quite often the truly original thinker or artist is met with skepticism or hostility by his contemporaries. Because they often push the boundaries of what is considered acceptable by less innovative members of their societies, creative individuals are often mocked, criticized, persecuted, or ignored during their lifetimes. As Kneller reminds us, Copernicus and Galileo were denounced as blasphemers and Stravinsky's "Right of Spring" nearly caused a riot. The poetry of Allen Ginsberg provoked a trial because it was considered obscene in the 1950s. Backlash is always the price that true innovators must pay for their art.

Interplay. Of course, there is nothing really totally new under the sun. Take the plots of any plays or novels or the subjects of any photograph or painting and you will probably find that it has all been done before. In some sense, the ability to create something truly novel—something out of nothing—is possible only for God. We puny human beings have to make do with relative novelty, which essentially involves the imaginative interplay of already existing elements. Although the pursuit of novelty in the truest sense of the world is probably a futile endeavor, this does not mean that there are not greater or lesser amounts of originality involved in human ideas and actions. We should, therefore, view creative activity on a spectrum in which radical innovation would be at the high end of the creative spectrum and, at the lower end, mere imitation or reproduction.

Utility. Finally, novelty and interplay alone do not make an act intrinsically creative. Appropriateness, relevance, and utility are also essential. The creative act, says Kneller, is always a response to a given situation; it must therefore "solve, or in some way clarify, the situation that has caused it to arise" (6). If our creative endeavors fail to serve some real need, satisfy an authentic interest, or solve some genuine problem, they will not resonate with anybody. Ginsberg's poetry, for example, touched his readers in the late 50s and early 60s because many of them were feeling suffocated by the sterile conformism of American society at the time. Ginsberg's decidedly non-conformist sensibilities as a writer spoke to the needs of young men and women who were tired of stale Eisenhower era sensibilities and who were looking for new ways to express the fears and anxieties that they had living in the post-war, nuclear age.

Can Creativity Be Learned?

Since this is a book about developing one's creative potential, it would seem obvious that we believe that every human being has the potential to become creative to one degree or another. But is this really such an obvious proposition? As the philosopher Richard Taylor has observed, the lives of so many people—perhaps even a majority of our fellow inhabitants on this planet—are so uninspired that it is extremely unlikely that they will create anything of worth in their lives. Think about the guy who works at some menial job during the day and who is more than content to spend his evenings swilling cheap beer and watching football. He may never even consider creating anything useful or interesting, and when he dies, Taylor argues, he will leave nothing behind worth remembering.

And this poor uninspired fellow is not alone. The world is filled with party queens and frat boys of all ages; all around us are men and women who live dull, insipid, and completely cosmetic, superficial lives. How many people can you think of right now who have created something novel, useful or interesting? Probably not very many, I would suspect.

Agreeing with Taylor, George Kneller argues that it is an illusion to think that everyone has the potential to become creative. Certain individuals, he maintains, possess a greater predisposition for creativity than others: "There seems to be no reason to believe...that nature is any more democratic in distributing creativity than she is in endowing intelligence. We accept a wide range of intelligence; why not of creativity?" Although he recommends that educators attempt to cultivate whatever latent creativity exists in children, and allow children the opportunity to attempt to express their creative gifts, the end results, he pragmatically warns, will remain unequal.

Although Taylor and Kneller may be correct when they maintain that most people will never be very creative in their lives, this does not mean that they lack the latent potential to be creative to one degree or another. As Chic Thompson so optimistically puts it:

> Creativity is not the exclusive domain of a few fortunate souls. Every person is creative, because creativity is one of the traits that makes us human. To be creative is to be able to perceive and recognize the world around us, to understand what we need or wish to do in response to it, and to set about changing it. To be creative is to find a way, a thought, an expression, a human manifestation no one has found and to make newly discovered possibilities reality (15).

To be creative is nothing more than to be fully human, totally alive. It means expressing your latent potential for self-discovery and self-revelation. And we are convinced that this is something that just about any serious person can achieve given the right conditions (proper motivation and a supportive, nurturing environment) and sufficient opportunities.

Although we argue that, like any other skill, creativity can be developed, this certainly does not mean that everyone will automatically become a creative genius in every field. In most cases, there may be a particular domain of creative expression that is more highly suited for some than others. I have seen students, for example, who wrote fairly feeble poetry, but whose visual sensibilities enabled them to shine in photography or art. The trick is to find that particular creative outlet that meshes well with the latent potential of each individual. And this means that people have to be exposed as early as possible to as many different creative outlets as possible in order to allow them the luxury of finding an area in which they can shine.

Furthermore, even in those cases where a person finds some specific area of creative expression in which he can excel, this does not automatically mean that he will necessarily be able to rise to the highest levels of excellence in that area. The simple truth is that creative genius has always been, and will always continue to be, extremely rare. Very few individuals, no matter how great their potentials or how strenuous their efforts, will ever be able to paint like Monet or write like James Joyce. They can, however, develop a significant amount of talent in a particular area of creative expression. And that in itself is quite an accomplishment.

This distinction between genius and talent has been summarized by Nathaniel Hirsh in his work *Genius and Creative Intelligence*. As Hirsh puts it:

> Geniuses themselves...know that they are not of the same breed as talented persons and are cognizant of the greater differences in relation to the talented than to any other group, including the peasant and the prince, the insane and the imbecile. By inherent nature they are antagonistic: the genius creates; the man of talent improves; the genius intuits, the man of talent analyzes and explores; the genius aspires, his life goal is creativity; the talented are animated by ambition and their life goal is power; the genius is ever a stranger in a strange land, a momentary sojourner in a strange interlude; the talented are those for whom the earth is paradise and social adjustment a natural and frictionless vocation. But the genius also has talent, and the development of his talent enables him to objectify his creativity and render it permanent. Genius with but little talent is like a great intellect with poor linguistic abilities; talent without genius is like a bright tongue attached to a feeble head. (cited in Arieti, 340-341).

In this program, I have absolutely no expectations that you will excel at everything you attempt or that, even in those areas where you do excel, you will rise to the level of genius. But I do anticipate that by the end of the 15 weeks of this program, you will be able to recognize those creative talents that lie within yourself and to develop them as fully as possible.

Your Creative Potential

Arguing that an individual's creative potential can be increased in no way means that everyone has exactly the same creative potential. Psychologist have determined that certain character traits are more closely associated with creative individuals than others (see Rogers, Kneller, Dacey). Those who possess traits such as openness to experience, tolerance for ambiguity, non-conformity, risk-taking, ability to focus, and some degree of basic intelligence seem to have an easier time maximizing their potentials for creativity than those who are lacking these traits.

If you want a sense of what your own creative potential might be, feel free to complete the survey on the following pages. A caveat, however, before you begin. There really is no absolute consensus on which traits are essential to creativity. Different theorists in the field of creative studies will list different traits they think are essential and the list is always evolving with new research. It should also be pointed out that, even if the traits listed earlier are in fact an accurate reflection of creative potential, there have been plenty of extremely creative individuals throughout history who completely lacked one or more of these traits (Most traditional icon painters, for exmaple, could hardly be called non-conformist, yet within the confines of their art, some were able to produce truly outstanding creative works). The survey should be used, therefore, not to put you into some kind of creative potential box, but as a tool for reflection on your own personality and the traits you possess that might help or hinder you on your quest to become more creative.

For Reflection

Creative Potential Survey

Instructions: Fill out this chart as honestly as possible. When you are finished, use the grading criteria on the next page to assess your own creative potential.

	Always	Frequently	Sometimes	Never
I display a great deal of curiosity about many things.		✓		
I am willing to take risks in life, even when doing so might cause me problems later on.			✓	
I freely express my opinions about a wide variety of topics.		✓	✓	
If I had to choose between being an explorer or a physician, I would rather be an explorer.		✓		
When I encounter a problem or difficulty, I don't stop until I find a solution.			✓	
I spend time fantasizing, daydreaming, or imagining.			✓	
I find humor in situations that are not always humorous to others; my sense of humor can appear bizarre or strange.	✓	✓		
I dislike having authority figures try to tell me what to do.			✓	
I am not afraid of contradiction and have been known to contradict myself or my own opinions on a subject.			✓	
I constantly ask questions about anything and everything.	✓	✓		
I am emotionally moved or inspired by beautiful things.		✓		
I am willing to accept failure as the price of trying to achieve something worthwhile.			✓	
When I am working on something that interests me, I become intensely focused and not easily distracted.		✓		
I have a high tolerance for ambiguity; I don't view life in "black and white" terms.		✓		
I have developed new ways for doing things.		✓		
I get a kick out of breaking the rules and doing things that I'm not supposed to.			✓	

I prefer highly unstructured environments or work situations to those that are highly structured.			✓	
I enjoy spending time by myself.	✓			
I am not afraid of making mistakes when trying something new.	✓			
I have the ability to stick with hard problems over extended periods of time.	✓			
My mind is filled with unconventional, weird, or provocative ideas.			✓	
I have a great deal of difficulty keeping my impulses under control.				✓
Given a choice between becoming economically successful or following my own dreams, I would choose the latter				
I have been known to get lost in my own thoughts and ideas.			✓	
I rarely see things in "black and white."	✓			

Grading the Survey

For each "always" answer give yourself 4 points, 3 points for "usually," 1 point for "sometimes," and 0 points for "never."

81-100: You definitely have the potential to become a creative person.

61-80: You have budding creative tendencies, but need to work on nurturing them.

51-60: You are in danger of stifling your creative potential by conforming far too much to the sterile dictates of the larger society. Begin to trust your own instincts a bit more and start spending time nurturing your creative side.

< 51: You would make a wonderful banker or accountant (Just kidding!). Take some more risks in life, broaden your horizons, do something creative to tap into the creative potential that all humans possess.

Express Yourself

The "Express Youself" exercises in this book provide you with the opportunity to write about the specific themes being discussed in each chapter. Over a period of 15 weeks you will be developing a creative portrait of youself that should capture the "real you." For now, however, we want to start nice and easy with some simple exercises aimed at getting you used to writing about yourself.

1.1. User Profile. You've probably created user profiles before when using popular web-based programs like Facebook or Twitter. A user profile is typically brief—about a paragraph or two—and tries to paint a sketch of who you are as an individual. Write one for yourself that get's to the essence of who you think you are. Try to have some fun with this: you can describe yourself any way you want, using whatever language you want.

This is only a first attempt to get a handle on who you are as a human being. You'll have plenty more opprtunities to develop some of the ideas you express in your user profile later on in the program. For now, just try to have some fun with this.

1.2. The Pivot Questionnaire. If you've ever watched "Inside the Actor's Studio," you probably look forward to the point in the show in which the host, James Lipton, asks a series of personal questions derived from Bernard Pivot's *Bouillion de Culture.* The reason that these questions are so interesting is that they get to the heart of who the person being interviewed actually is. Try answering these questions yourself, but make sure to explain the rationale behind you answers:

- What is your favorite word?
- What is your least favorite word?
- What turns you on creatively, spiritually, or emotionally?
- What turns you off?
- What is your favorite curse word?
- What sound or noise do you love?
- What sound or noise do you hate?
- What profession other than your own would you like to attempt?
- What profession would you not like to do?
- If heaven exists, what would you like to hear God say when you arrive at the Pearly Gates?

1.3. I the Expert. This is a great exercise to get you started on your writing, because everyone is an expert at something. Just pick some activity that you know how to do well and simply explain in as clear a manner as possible how to do it. This doesn't have to be anything extremely interesting. You can describe how to make the perfect cup of coffee, how to tie your shoe laces, how to dress for success, how to have a perfect bowel movement, how to offend people at a social gathering, or anything else you think you're an expert at.

1.4. Anytime Writing. Anytime writing is just that: it's writing you can do any time during the course of the next 16 weeks. Here's how it works: as things surface in your life that are significant to you, explore them in as much detail as possible and then write about them. You don't have to worry about how profound or interesting your writing is, or what other people might think about what you've written. Just get it down on paper. Later on you will have ample time to rework what you've written.

1.4.1. What's Going On? Take an experience from the past week that was personally significant to you and write about it. Again, this doesn't have to be a ground-shaking or life-altering event—just an experience that makes some kind of impression upon you. Describe the event as vividly as possible.

1.4.2. What's on Your Mind? This is similar to the "What's Going On" writing, except that, rather than focusing on what you are doing, you focus on what you are thinking. What's been on your mind lately? What preoccupies your thoughts? Now write about it.

1.4.3. What are You Feeling? The best writing comes from the guts—from that place deep inside you where emotions spring forth. Perhaps you've been experiencing a strong emotional reaction to a specific event in your life. Take the time to feel this emotion intimately and then write about it as honestly as possible.

Remember, these anytime writing exercises can be returned to as often as you'd like throughout the 16 weeks of this program. Part of what you are going to be doing in this program is to try to become more attuned to significant experiences, thoughts, and feelings in your life, to reflect deeply upon them, and then to write about them in as much detail as possible. So, if things pop up in your daily life that make an impression upon you, don't hesitate to shift your attention to them.

POST
NO
BILLS

2

Impediments To Creativity

It has been argued by Carl Rogers that the desire to create is part of man's innate need to actualize himself, to achieve his full potential in life. Rogers goes on to describe this tendency as "the directional trend which is evident in all organic and human life—the urge to expand, extend, develop, mature—the tendency to express and activate all the capacities of the organism, to the extent that such activation enhances the organism or the self." He also believes that, although this tendency may be buried or hidden in some individuals, it exists in everyone and needs only the proper conditions in order to be activated (72).

Indeed it does seem that human beings are naturally creative to one degree or another. In fact, some of the earliest artifacts of our primitive ancestors are cave paintings that serve no practical purpose. Although life in prehistoric times was a daily struggle for survival, it seems that human beings nonetheless felt compelled to express themselves creatively. Children also seem to have a natural desire to play, create, and imagine— until these healthy tendencies are stamped out of them by their parents and the educational establishment.

If it's true that human beings are naturally creative, then why do so few people engage in creative endeavors? And why aren't you exercising your natural creative potential right now? There may be several different causes at work, but there are three fallacious attitudes in particular that seem to prevent most people from undertaking creative projects.

"I Don't Deserve to Be Creative"

The most common response that I receive from students about why they don't attempt creative activities is that they really do believe that that sort of thing is reserved exclusively for an elite who are privileged enough to be anointed as artists. They may want to attempt to write a novel or make a short film, but don't believe they are creative enough to attempt such projects. Art, music, and creative writing, we are told, are the realm of great talents, and we are often taught to believe that it's almost sacrilegious for us to even think of trodding on the same ground as Monet, Beethoven, or Tolstoy.

We may never actually hear anyone say something like, "Who are you to think that you can write a novel," but we know that is what the so-called authorities think. If you don't belong to the right creative club from an exceptionally early age, you might as well give up all thought of even trying anything creative.

I remember a story a student, Eddie, told me once that is probably fairly typical of what most people have to go through when they first attempt to be creative. He was watching TV in the living room and his parents were in the kitchen talking. He remembered hearing his mother say to his father, "This is a picture that Eddie painted today at school." It was a painting he had spent considerable time and energy on and he was proud of it. His father—probably never assuming that he would overhear—replied matter-of-factly, "Well, he'll certainly never make a living doing that." Perhaps Eddie's father was simply referring to how difficult it was at the time for artists to earn a decent living, but Eddie, of course, took this to be a slight on his abilities as a painter and never seriously picked up a brush again.

Rejection is common in every creative field. All great artists, photographers, writers, and film-makers at one point or another during their careers are inevitably told that they lack the talent necessary to succeed in their chosen fields. Vincent Van Gogh heard this refrain his entire life, and never really knew artistic success while he lived. Van Gogh, however, perservered in his art, despite all the rejection he received. How many budding artists and writers are there in the world, however, who completely give up the attempt to be creative because they think they lack the "stuff" neccessary to succeed?

"Everyone Has to Be Productive All The Time"

If you are an American, you were born and raised in an environment which has directly or indirectly conditioned you to believe that the only activities worth investing your time and energy in are those which will reap the most financial reward for you. From your earliest days, you were probably taught to work hard in order to make a success of yourself, and by the time you became a young adult you were probably discouraged from engaging in "frivolous" activities (playing, doodling, goofing off, or just hanging out) that seemed to serve no practical function.

This fundamental American attitude which suggests that most of our waking hours should be spent working and being "productive" has become known as the Protestant Work Ethic, but basically it is the underlying creed of the American capitalist system. This system judges individuals not on how happy, creative, or free they are, but on how much money and stuff they have managed to amass in their lifetimes.

In a system like this, the most useless people are those who spend their time engaged in idle thoughts (philosophers) or who produce things that cannot easily be sold at a profit (artists). Naturally, those who spent too much time involved in creative endeavors like painting or creative writing are viewed either with suspicion, bewilderment, or even hostility by the more "practical" people around them.

If you think that what I have just said is a gross exaggeration, answer these three questions:

- When was the last time you spent several hours engaged in any sort of activity that could be described as creative? What was the attitude of the people around you?
- What would happen if you started doodling or writing poetry at home for an extended period of time? Would you be praised for exercising your creative potential?
- What would happen if you told your family members that you were planning to take up painting or acting just for fun and you would be spending about seven hours per week—which amounts to only one hour per day—working on your new pastime?

Most people who answer these questions honestly would probably have to admit that our society as a whole is not particularly receptive or encouraging to those who attempt to be more creative. If you come from a family or a community in which creative enterprises are supported, then consider yourself lucky. You are definitely in a privileged minority.

"Everything I Do Has to be Perfect"

The final great curse that stands in the way of attempting anything creative is an attitude of perfectionism that often makes us not want to take on new projects unless we think that we can do them better than anyone else.

The perfectionist in us is always telling us that unless we can do things flawlessly, we shouldn't do them at all.

Naturally, there is absolutely nothing wrong with trying to produce the best work you can or attempt to do something better than others have done it before. It's precisely that kind of attitude that makes for great artists, thinkers, and inventors. The problem with perfectionism is that it is often used as a shield to protect us from the criticism of others. If we don't produce anything because nothing will be perfect enough, we don't ever have to worry about people criticizing, challenging, or belittling us for what we do.

The fear of criticism becomes particularly acute when it relates to work done by artists or other creative people, because, as Edward Kurpis points out, the act of creating something

> is usually a powerful representation of oneself. Artists and creators in all fields often seek a measure of personal fulfillment, recognition or admiration through their private efforts and expressions of art. Seeking that kind of acceptance from those efforts is fraught with potentially devastating consequences, particularly if the need for such reinforcement is meaningful to the artist (21).

Unlike some other activities, the act of creating is also uniquely personal. The artist, writer, film-maker, or photographer always puts a little piece of himself into everything that he creates—and sometimes a very big piece. When a creative work is criticized, it often seems like a personal rejection. If we create nothing, then our work won't be criticized and our fragile egos get to remain intact.

Overcoming the Impediments to Creativity

So, if these attitudes are what prevent many people from trying to be more creative, what can be done—if anything—to remove these sorts of motivational impediments? From my own experience, I've noticed that students who tend to be the most fearless creators tend to adopt four key dispositions that enable them to keep creating, despite any lack of support or encouragement they might receive from those around them.

1. Nurturing a Sense of Creative Self-Entitlement

While we might not think we have the right to be creative, in fact, as Dave Storer points out, creativity is the birthright of every human being. "We are all born," he writes, " with incredible creative abilities, and few things in life make us happier than fully engaging those abilities. To let a belief that we haven't the proper "permission"—from either society, family and friends, or ourselves—stop us from developing and expressing our deepest, truest selves in the best creative way we know how would be a terrible loss" (12). The choice to create or not to, he reminds us, is ours and ours alone. No one can or should be able to deprive us of this most basic right to express ourselves.

If you start to doubt yourself, just repeat the following mantra about ten, fifty, or one hundred times. Keep repeating it until you actually become convinced that what you are repeating to yourself is the gospel truth:

> *I have the right to be creative!*
> *I have the ability to be creative!*
> *And, damn it, I will be creative no matter what anyone else says!*

2. *Jumping Right In*

Once you convince yourself that you have the right to express yourself creatively, the next step is to jump right in and try working in a medium that has always interested you. The choice of the particular creative venue to try will vary from person to person, but there is certainly at least one area that you can explore. If you enjoy writing, try poetry, drama, creative fiction, or screenplay writing. If you are more visually oriented, you might attempt photography, videography, or painting. The choice is totally up to you.

Then, just pick up the brush, or the pen, or the camera and start playing. You don't have to accomplish anything or even produce anything of worth. Just enjoy youself.

Some people may prefer to take a more intellectual approach and investigate the works of great artists in books, museums or on the web. That's perfectly fine too. Just don't spend all your time reading, and don't forget that the point here is to actually create something. Above all else, don't think that anything you produce will have to reach the level of excellence achieved by the creative masters that you are investigating. Your job is to get inspired and start creating. That's it.

3. *Embracing Imperfectionism*

The overemphasis on perfectionism, as we have seen, can prove an impediment to undertaking any sort of creative endeavor. So what is the budding creator to do in order to overcome his or her fear of not being an immediate creative master? The first step is to give yourself complete and total permission to fail at anything you attempt. All the great creative geniuses throughout history have failed at one point or another and some have failed repeatedly. What made them unique is that they didn't allow failure to stop them from creating.

Our own motto in the program is that to fail is to succeed, because if you are failing you are at least attempting to do something creative. On the other hand, if you play it safe all the time, you may never fail at what you attempt, but you will probably never produce anything really outstanding either.

One solution to get over your fear of failure and overcome your perfectionist tendencies is to actively cultivate a joy in doing things really, really badly—to embrace, in other words, the joy of imperfectionism. This may seem like a strange attitude to adopt, but it actually can be quite liberating. As Edward Kurpis advises:

> Give yourself permission to do "bad work." Not everything you create needs to be Mozart, Monet, or Mamet. In fact, set out to be the *anti-master*. Be messy on purpose; intend to write bad poetry; make a soufflé and then jump around your kitchen to make sure it falls. In other words, as an exercise, strive to be human. Most importantly, share these failures with everyone you know. Just don't tell them you failed on purpose. Have a few good private laughs as you put everyone in the uncomfortable position of examining the worst of your worst. Feel what it feels like to hear the less than perfect reactions you get—and not care about what's being said—since you directed this experiment. Do this until you develop the understanding that you can divorce yourself from the harsh reactions of others (Kurpis, 22-23).

In fact, some fairly significant artists have built their entire careers out of producing utter and complete shit and calling it art. John Lennon and his wife Yoko Ono produced no fewer than three albums that are considered virtually unlistenable, not only by music critics, but also by some of Lennon's most hardcore fans. And the filmmaker John Waters produced a string of ridiculously bad films, like *Pink Flamingos* and *Polyester* which went on to become cult classics.

4. Cultivating Wildness

In his work, *Fearless Creating*, Eric Maisel argues that in order to be truly creative one must first learn to cultivate a sense of wildness. "This wildness," he says, "has many faces." It is an amalgam of passion, vitality, rebelliousness, non-conformity, freedom from inhibitions" (12). In order to cultivate the kind of wildness that will fuel your creative tendencies, Maisel argues that you've got to get over your inhibitions, tameness, and conformism and tap into the adventurous, reckless, passionate side of your nature. A wild man or woman exists inside all of us, but quite often we are too timid or self-conscious to let him or her come out.

Although you can create art without cultivating any sense of wildness at all, the art that you do create will probably be so tepid and sterile that it won't even inspire yourself, let alone anyone else. A life without wildness in general might suit an accountant or stockbroker, but if you are like most people, tapping into the inner wild man or woman that exists in all of us can only make life richer and more rewarding. I'm not advising you to go crazy, or to act in a way that would endanger yourself or others, but certainly you could conceive of spending an hour or two a week trying to break free of the sterile conformism that is expected by the larger society.

Exercise

In Fearless Creating, *Eric Maisel asks us to reflect on how wildness manifests itself in our own lives. When, where or how do you reveal your own wild face?*

- work when ts craze

- Bot comp

-

-

-

How easy was it for you to think about instances where you show your wild face in life? If it was difficult to think of any times at all when you bucked convention and did something purely spontaneous or unconventional, then you may want to reflect upon what's holding you back.

In this program, you are constantly going to be encouraged to become a bit of a rebel, to delight in your own creative genius, to pursue your passions wherever they might ultimately lead (within reason, of course!). If you do this, even to a limited degree, you might just find that your innate creative energies suddenly become unleashed. And you'll probably also find that your life in general becomes a heck of a lot more interesting as a result.

Express Yourself

Once again we are going to focus on simple writing exercises that get you comfortable expressing yourself in written form. This week, you can write about anything on your mind and express yourself using any form you desire (descriptive prose, poetry, story-telling, dialogue, etc.). Just write about what interests you and write for yourself. Leave your internal critic behind (you can always pick him up again later on!).

2.1. All Blocked Up. Think about a time when you felt blocked. This blockage could be physical, intellectual, emotional, spiritual, interpersonal or creative. Perhaps it was a time when you felt blocked from becoming the kind of person you wanted to be. Describe what caused this feeling of blockage, how you felt about it, and how you eventually dealt with it.

2.2. The Three Impediments. Go back and reread the pages on the three impediments to creativity described in this chapter. Have you ever experienced any of these in your own life? If so, write about it.

2.3. Permission to Be Very Bad. As we have seen, part of what prevents people from undertaking creative endeavors is the fear of looking bad. To help you get over this, you now have permission to do some creative act very badly. For example, write a REALLY bad poem or story. Or do something really badly and write about how it feels. Have fun with this!

2.4. Your Wild Face. Go back to the exercise on the previous page and select one time when you let your wild face show in life. Describe what caused you to go wild, how you felt doing it, and what the consequences were of bucking the status quo.

2.5. Automatic Writing (for those with serious writer's block). If you find yourself completely incapable of writing about anything at all, try this exercise: Set timer for five minutes, take out a pen and some paper, and simply write about whatever comes into your mind, no matter how strange or incoherent it might seem. When five minutes is up, you have your piece of writing. We'll be returning to various forms of automatic writing throughout this program, because it has been used by many writers to free up the mind and to overcome self-consciousness in writing.

2.6. Anytime Writing. Remember, you can return to the "Anytime Writing" exercises in Chapter 1 as often as you like.

3

Eyes Wide Open

There's an old saying that we look, but often do not see; we hear, but frequently fail to listen. When was the last time you slowed down enough to actually notice a rosebud just beginning to open in the springtime, or stopped to feel the cool morning breeze against your skin when you went to go out to get the morning newspaper?

Although we perform a great many activities in life, we often don't take the time to really notice many of the amazing things going on right in front of our noses. Your goal this week is to begin to become a detailed observer whose mission is to penetrate to the essence or vital core of things.

The main technique that we will cultivate is what is often referred to as concentrated awareness. This sort of practice has been used for centuries—mainly in Eastern cultures—as a basic tool for meditative practice, but we will use it as a vehicle for beginning to look at the world around us in a deeper, more penetrative way. The goal is to get beyond the world that you typically perceive—a world where things are usually seen in a perpetual state of flux, always changing, fleeting, and impermanent, to reach the essence of things as they are in themselves.

This state of concentrated awareness is often difficult to achieve, because we rarely take the time in our daily lives to stop running around and become more mindful. Fortunately, there are a few common techniques that can help us to achieve the state of concentrated awareness that is so vital for any sort of creative activity.

Awareness of the Breath

In Buddhist meditative practice the oldest technique for attaining a state of concentrated awareness is to begin by focusing on something so close to us that we often forget about it—our breath. The reason that the breath is often used as an object of contemplation in most Eastern traditions is that it is always with us and, therefore, readily available as an object of contemplation.

In Buddhist practice the focus on the breath as an object of contemplation is also referred to as "calm abiding" or "single-pointed concentration." The goal of this practice ultimately is to be able to hold our minds on a single object of meditation—in this case, the flow of the breath as it moves in and out of our bodies—and to be able to remain in this state for as long as we wish. If this sounds easy, it most certainly is not. In fact, many people who initially take up meditation describe this practice as one of the most difficult things they have ever attempted in their lives. Indeed, to reach a state of concentrated awareness in which the mind is stable and able to focus on any object even for a few minutes at a time takes quite a bit of practice, and for many people is often a life-long pursuit.

To start, let's just try to focus on the in and out flow of your breath for a period of about 5 minutes. Here are the basics of the practice:

- Sit in a comfortable position with eyes closed. Take a few deep breaths and relax your body. Notice the breaths as they enter and leave your body and try for three minutes to focus on nothing but these breaths.
- If thoughts about anything pop up in your mind as you do this exercise, just take note of them. As the thoughts arise try to label them as specifically as possible: i.e., thinking about the pain in my shoulder, nervous about upcoming exam, feeling angry about X.
- Then gently try to return your mind to your breathing.
- If the practice is too difficult at first, you can count breaths… One on the in-breath, two on the out-breath and so on…You can also focus on the in-breaths and out-breaths, noting "breathing-in, breathing out."

In a more advanced version of this practice, you would observe not just the breath in general, but also attempt to focus on the specific quality of each breath, noting whether your breath is short or long, shallow or deep.

You might also focus on each specific movement of the breath, noting the quality of the in-breath as the air moves through your nasal passages and into your lungs, the pause between the in- and out-breath, and the out-breath, as the air moves out of your lungs. What you would discover, if you did this for long enough, is that something as seemingly uninteresting as your breath is actually quite fascinating and complex.

If you are like most people, you probably found this practice, as simple as it is, amazingly frustrating. As you tried to focus on your breath, your mind almost certainly went wandering all over the place and you probably found it difficult to concentrate, even for the few minutes you did this exercise. This is perfectly natural. Most experienced meditators would advise you to try to be as gentle as possible with yourself when your mind wanders from its object of contemplation. If distractions persist, take a few deep breaths, gently note the distracting thought, and return to your breathing. Above all, don't try to force the mind, or attempt to stop thinking entirely, both of which are exercises in futility. As Zen master Shunryu Suzuki advises,

> When you are practicing [concentrated awareness] do not try to stop your thinking. Let it stop by itself. If something comes into your mind, let it come in and go out, it will not stay long. When you try to stop your thinking, it means you are bothered by it. Do not be bothered by anything. It appears that the something comes from outside your mind, but actually it is only the waves of your mind and if you are not bothered by waves, gradually they will become calmer and calmer…Many sensations come, many thoughts or images arise but they are just waves from your own mind. Nothing comes from outside your own mind…If you leave your mind as it is, it will become calm. This mind is called big mind (34).

Another common mistake that would-be meditators make is to judge what comes up during the process of concentrating on the breath as either good or bad. There is absolutely no other goal in this practice than simply being fully present to the breath and whatever comes up during the practice. Whether you slip into ecstatic rapture while concentrating on your breath or whether your mind is screaming out in boredom from the seeming monotony of the experience, your job is simply to note what you are experience without judgment and return to the breath. If you feel that you can't refrain from judging the quality of your experience, then simply note the fact that you are judging and then return to the breath.

Awareness of Routine Activity

The breathing exercise described above is an important foundation for developing concentrated awareness in other areas of your life. In theory, you should be able to perform any practice with complete and total awareness.   As a foundation for increasing awareness of the routine activities in your daily life, try the following "raisin exercise," modified from Jon Kabat-Zinn's work, *Full Catastrophe Living*:

- Holding. Take a raisin out of its box and hold it in your hand, feeling the weight of the raisin as it sits in your palm or between your fingers.
- Seeing. Look at the raisin, examining each and every part of it in intimate detail and noting its colors and surfaces.   Examine the raisin as though you have never seen one before.
- Touching. Place the raisin between your fingers, exploring its texture. If it helps, you can close your eyes as you do this.
- Smelling. Hold the raisin beneath your nose, and take in its fragrance.
- Placing. Slowly lift the raisin to your mouth and place it on your tongue without chewing it. Spend a few moments feeling the sensation of the raisin in your mouth.
- Tasting. When you are ready to chew the raisin, place it between your teeth, and then very slowly and consciously take a bite. Without swallowing the raisin, notice the sensations that arise as well as any changes that occur over time. As you chew some more, notice the changes that take place in the shape and texture of the raisin.
- Swallowing. When you are ready, make an intention to swallow the raisin and then follow it as it passes down your throat and into your esophagus.
- Noting. Note how your body feels as a result of this exercise in mindful eating (27-28).

If you happen to have a dislike for raisins, you can do this exercise with just about any food item. The key is to place your full attention on the food item you are eating so that you are completely and totally mindful about what you are doing. If stray thoughts enter your mind as you are doing this exercise, note them, and gently return your full attention to what you are eating.

You can also apply the same principles of mindful awareness to any other daily activity—brushing your teeth, driving to work, going to the bathroom. For example, if you are washing the dishes, give your full, complete, and total attention to what you are doing. Notice the way your hands feel in the water, how the suds feel on your hands, the sensation of rubbing the dishes and rinsing them off.

Why are practices like these so important, you might be wondering? The answer is that to the extent that we are fully alive, we are also fully engaged in the present moment. Not in the past, which is already gone; not in future, which may never come; not in some fantasy realm, which doesn't really exist. To live is to BE HERE NOW, doing whatever it is we are doing with total attentiveness.

Being attentive to the present moment in whatever form it takes is also essential to just about any creative endeavor you can imagine. Whether you are painting, writing, editing a film, or just doing macramé, if you are fully engaged in what you are doing—not trapped in the past or the future or some fantasyland of your own imagination—you are much more likly to succeed in producing something creative.

From Experience to Self-Expression

Look around you. Notice what's in front of you. Now concentrate on it, experience it fully, completely, totally. It doesn't matter whether you are gazing at a sunset on the beach, staring at your face in the mirror, listening to someone talk about his problems, or pulling weeds. Whatever you are doing, no matter how mundane, you can use the principles of concentrated awareness to focus your mind and begin to see things as they really are.

If you talked to a Zen Buddhist monk, he would probably tell you that simply using a method like concentrated awareness to become fully present to the world around you is the first and last step on the road to enlightenment. To the extent that you are present and mindfully aware of what's going on around you, you are also fully alive as a human being. For our purposes in this creativity program, however, something more is required. Not only do we have to learn to see things around us as they are in themselves—in all their splendor, brilliance, and wonder—but we also have to learn to communicate what we experience in an interesting and artful manner.

Think of what you are experiencing—whether it is a sunset at the end of the day, playtime with a young child, the pitter-patter of raindrops falling on your window pane—as the raw material, the building-blocks, of your potential creative endeavors. All you have to do is take what you have experienced through the act of concentrated awareness and do something fun with it.

Let's see how the process of using concentrated awareness might work when applied to a simple writing exercise. A 20-year-old college student named Keisha walks outside her house one morning. Attempting to take the idea of concentrated awareness seriously, she spends a few moments looking at the wonderful orange coneflowers that her father planted in front of her house several years ago. They have been coming up faithfully every spring and adding a splash of brilliant color to her garden, but she rarely had taken the time to notice them at all. Now she studies them with all the intensity that she can possibly muster, noting the various shades of orange in the flower, the specific curvature of each petal, and the tiny protruding seeds in the cone itself. Then she smells the flower, detecting just a slight hint of sweet honey-like fragrance. She touches the petals, noting their smooth, silky texture and then the cone, feeling its rough, bumpy surface. After several minutes of using all of her senses to examine the flower, Keisha takes out her trusty pad and pencil—she always carries these with her wherever she goes—and begins to allow all of her thoughts and feelings about the flower to pour out on paper in a stream-of-consciousness fashion:

Stream-of-Consciousness Post
By Keisha Johnson

dad's damn flowers – his pride and joy, but they leave me completely cold – so totally and completely boring – I have more important things to think about in my life – got to do it anyway, so I bite the bullet and take some time to allow the old senses to experience them – start with the visual – smooth orange petals surrounding bumpy seeds – skinny, tall stems that almost seem too weak to support such fat flowers – now the smell – honey fragrance – so incredibly sweet – like morning marmalade on crispy toast -- bumpy shell --- I take you in my mouth and spit out – uuuuuggggg – coneflowers look good but taste like hell – bees buzzing all around – hope they don't sting me, the little bastards – I hate bees – don't think much of flowers either, but at least this one is pretty – I wish I was that pretty – pretty as a coneflower in spring – but even the coneflower will look like garbage in a few weeks – that's just the way life works, I guess – there's that bee again – if he stings me I'm going to scream – back to the coneflower – dad calls it Echinacea, like the stuff people take when they are sick – is that the same thing? – remember to ask him about that – can't think of anything else to write about this stupid flower – nothing to say, nothing to say, nothing to say – what would spring be like if there were no flowers blooming? – would anybody even notice?

Now Keisha has the raw data that she needs to turn her observations of reality into some kind of creative work. What will she do with all of this information?

She decides to start by simply writing about the experience of leaving her house and noticing the coneflowers for the first time. Right now, she's not overly worried about how her writing sounds or if her observations are profound. She simply wants to describe an experience as simply and honestly as possible, in as much detail as possible. At the same time, she is trying to capture all of her reactions to what she is experiencing, so that a potential reader would almost feel as though he is sharing in the same experience with her.

Coneflower Confessional
By Keisha Johnson

I have a confession to make. In the 18 years that I have been living on this planet, I haven't spent two minutes thinking about flowers. I know that there must be a million flowers blooming every time I walk down my street, but they never really seemed all that interesting to me. I mean, global warming, getting a decent job after college, and having enough money to enjoy myself on the weekends—these are important things to me. The wonders of nature, quite frankly, leave me cold.

Maybe I'm just reacting to my father's fanatical interest in gardening. The guy seems to center his entire existence around how his damned perennials are doing. Whenever he starts going off on how beautiful his flowers are, I almost always want to take a very long sleep. It would also bring him wild joy if I took any kind of interest in his favorite hobby, so you can be sure, for that reason alone, I would never give his garden the time of day.

But now I have no choice, I have to find some object in the yard to practice concentrated awareness on, and the ridiculous coneflowers in front of the house seem like a decent place to start. So I stumble out of the house, and crouch down at eye level with my father's favorite orange coneflower—or Echinacea as he calls it. I heard him babble on about the amazing medicinal properties of this plant, but right now I can't seem to remember what kinds of ailments it's supposed to cure....Probably not herpes (Okay. That one was way out of line!).

Despite my apathy towards flowers, I have to admit that this particular coneflower is kind of amazing. I like the way it stands so regally straight up in the air, showing off its long petals like some kind of egomaniacal prom queen. The luscious orange color of the petals really is quite beautiful (I wish I had hair that color!). Moving as close as I can to the center of the cone, I notice all the bumpy little seeds—so rough compared to the silkiness of the petals.

I was almost getting into the experience of communing with nature, when a nasty bee buzzes by my head. I hate fucking bees! This one is definitely trying to warn me away from the coneflower, like some kind of jealous lover. I don't blame him at all. If I were as pretty as the coneflower, I'd have all sorts of interesting suitors buzzing around me too.

It strikes me, though, that in a short while, this flower will be all dried up and withered. Nothing beautiful lasts forever, I suppose. Perhaps that's why it's so important to appreciate beautiful things while you have them.

Maybe I did learn something worthwhile from this idiot exercise after all!

Certainly, there's nothing very original or profound about this little piece. It's a fairly literal account of Keisha's sensory interaction with the coneflower. But something interesting came out of it. Rather than simply describing the flower, Keisha has used the experience as a jumping off point for talking about her ambivalent feelings towards her father, her own desires (to be more attractive and to find a decent suitor), and her fears about nature (the bee). More interesting still, she has begun the more difficult process of using a fairly ordinary experience to reflect upon the transitory nature of human life itself. Not too shabby for a first attempt at self-expression!

There are plenty of other ways that the experience of interacting with a coneflower could be transformed into something creative. After completing her stream-of-consciousness post and her descriptive essay, Keisha goes on to create a poem that takes some of the themes in her earlier writing exercises and moves them in a more fanciful direction. Then she goes on to write a fictitious dialogue between herself and the rejected lover as well as a bit of flash fiction story-telling with a revenge angle.   When she is finished writing, she uses the same coneflower as the subject of a photograph and a sketch.

All in all, Keisha will have used a fairly simple experience as a foundation to create six different types of creative product. For a person normally not interested in creative self-expression, this is actually a fairly impressive achievement. But Keisha couldn't have produced any of these interesting creative works had she not first taken the time to concentrate on the world around her and attempted to capture her experience in as vivid detail as possible.

The point that I am trying to make here is that there is no limit to the number of creative possibilities that you can pursue once you let your creative juices start flowing. The first step, however, is to take the time to open your eyes and start seeting things around you in all their glory and magesty.

For Reflection

1. What other sorts of creative ventures do you think Keisha could have pursued using her experience with the conflowers (try to think outside the box when coming up with possible projects)?

   wet the petals
   press b/t wax paper - iron on her
   to iron = clothing

2. What are some ordinary, seemingly boring objects that you regularly *encounter* or *use* in your daily life that could be possible objects of creative inspiration (Stretch your imagination here!)?

   Stethoscope
   Small plunger (yellow)
   rolling pin

3. What are some ordinary, seemingly boring things that you *do* every day that could also inspire your creative imagination (Again, try to be imaginative with this)?

   bake
   clean

Express Yourself

The exercises during our second week of this program focus on using the method of concentrated awareness that we discussed in this chapter as a vehicle for creative expression. The key to all these exercises is to take the time to begin to notice the things about which you are planning to write. Be sure to employ ALL of your senses during the process of examining the world around you and try to be as descriptive as possible in your writing.

As always, you can take these writing exercises in whatever direction you want. If you feel stuck, go back and work on some of the exercises that you skipped from chapters one or two, or write about some topic that is more interesting to you. There are no rules here: just helpful suggestions.

3.1. Natural Wonders. There is a world of wonders right outside your front door, but you may not even know they're there. Open up that door... then open up your eyes and report what you see.

3.1.1. Take a walk outside your house. Find some object of natural beauty, observe it carefully for at least a few minutes, noting all its details. Write about the object in prose or poetry in a way that gives the reader a true sense of what the natural object is like.

3.1.2. Go outside in your backyard and lay on the grass, observing the sky intently for at least a few minutes. Note every detail about the sun, the clouds, the colors that you can. Now write about what you've observed.

3.1.3. Go out into your backyard and notice all the natural wonders around you during the particular season in which you are writing. Write about the natural objects you see as though you are looking at them for the first time.

3.2 Nature Haikus. For several centuries in Japan there was a tradition of writing haikus to capture a specific moment or experience. A haiku is a three-lined poem in which the first and last lines have five syllables and the middle line has seven. The 5-7-5 form of the haiku is traditional, but is certainly not sacrosanct (the specific number of syllables in each line can be modified slightly). Traditionally haikus also have no rhyme scheme, minimal punctuation, and do not use titles. In order to give a sense of immediacy, haikus are also typically written in the present tense. The following haiku, written by the Japanese poet Matsuo Bahso, clearly illustrates all these features:

An old pond

a frog jumps in
Sound of water

Haikus are deceptively simple forms of poetry. In fact, to write an excellent haiku, you need to observe the object about which you are writing very carefully and with a certain cool detachment. You also have to develop an ability to relate an experience in a very clear and concise manner, which is quite difficult for many writers. All in all, haikus represent an excellent opportunity to translate some of the ideas we have been discussing about concentrated awareness into written form.

For this exercise, all you have to do is find some place where there are some beautiful—or at least interesting—things for you to observe. A park, a nature preserve, the beach, or even your backyard would be fine. Then focus on a few natural objects that capture your attention and try your hand at writing some haikus of your own.

3.3. The Open Drawer or Closet. Open up any drawer of your dresser and write about what you encounter as you rummage through it. Describe not only the items that you encounter, but also how you feel about these items.

3.4. The Extraordinary Ordinary. Find some object in your house or garage that you use every day (the more boring it is, the better) and study this object for as long as you can, looking at it as though you are seeing it for the first time. Now write about that object in as much detail as possible.

3.5. Eye Spy. Go to some public place (a park, a busy street corner, a supermarket, a train station, a bookstore, a library, etc) and simply observe what is going on in that environment. Note what kinds of people are present, what they look like, what sorts of things they are saying, what you think or feel about them.

3.6. In the Bathroom. Take an activity you normally do while in the bathroom, and make a conscious effort to pay close attention as your perform this activity. Now write about this in detail.

3.7. Getting Dressed. Observe in detail everything that you do when you are getting dressed in the morning. Describe in as much detail as possible, all the steps involved in getting yourself dressed. Make sure not to leave anything out, no matter how insignificant it might seem.

3.8. Along the Way. On your way to work or school, note at least three things that you typically see every day that you don't usually take notice of (e.g., the street light, the corner gas station, the old 7-11, your rear view mirror). Choose one to examine in detail and write about. Feel free to use your imagination when writing this piece.

4

Special Somethings

In the previous chapter we saw that just about any object—no matter how mundane it might appear to you at first glance—can become a source of creative inspiration if you just take the time to explore this thing in all its miraculous diversity. After all, how many still-life bowls of fruit do you find gracing the major museums of the world? If an artist can find something sublime about objects as innocuous as plums and apricots, then this clearly indicates that the source of inspiration lies in the artist him or herself, rather than in any object he or she chooses to focus upon.

We saw, for example, that Keisha had no particular attachment to the coneflowers in front of her house. In fact, you could say that she had something of an aversion towards them because she resented her father's obsession with these flowers. Still, when asked to apply the method of concentrated awareness, she was able to rise above her apathy and find the miraculous in the mundane. If our minds are open enough, then theoretically any object, experience, person or memory can become a treasure trove for creative inspiration.

Of course, there are certain objects that seem to almost automatically inspire us. Let us call these "objects of special significance," or, better still, "special somethings." The stuffed teddy bear that you had as a child growing up, for example, might be a special something for you. But what is it that makes this teddy bear more significant, for example, than a similar stuffed animal that you also had as a child, but which now is relegated to a musty box in the basement with other forgotten mementos? Why does the teddy bear still occupy a place of honor on your bed years after you supposedly have outgrown the need for such childish toys?

The answer is that the teddy bear, for one reason or another, has been granted the status of a special something by you, whereas the toys that you boxed in the basement, gave away to younger siblings, or simply tossed in the trash never received such status. These other less significant toys are just things with no sentimental value or significance, and so parting with them is really not very painful at all. But the teddy bear is different. If someone cleaning your room accidentally threw out the teddy bear, thinking it was just a silly, insignificant object that you no longer needed, you'd probably be horrified.

But what is it that gives Teddy such special significance?

What Makes a Thing "Special"?

The answer is that you have bestowed upon him two qualities that most other objects in your life fail to possess—affection and fondness. Looking at the roots of these words helps flesh out why special somethings play such an important role in our lives. The word "affection" comes, like so many words in our language from the Latin "*afficere*" (to affect) and can literally be defined as "the state of being moved or acted upon." Our special somethings, then, have been invested with such significance that they affect our emotional states: we desire them when we don't have them, feel pain or fear when they are missing, and experience pleasure when they are in our presence. Most other objects we use in our lives—the refrigerator, the television, the can opener—completely lack the emotional quality that we've bestowed upon these special somethings.

If you think that no object can possibly be that significant in our lives, think again. The fondness we have for certain possessions cuts to the very core of our personal identity. Indeed, the word "fond" comes from the Latin word *fundus*, meaning bottom and the French word *fond*, meaning source, foundation or core. As the roots of the word indicate, the often-passionate connection that we have for the special somethings in our lives affects us to the very core of our being. Our relationship to these things, believe it or not, helps shape who we are as human beings.

The example of the teddy bear is typical for many people because it is so laden with emotional baggage from childhood, but we can bestow affection and fondess on virtually any object in our lives. Many men, for example, seem particularly attached to their cars. If you tried to tell them that a car is just a thing that can be replaced, more than a few men would probably take issue with you. The Prada pocketbook that you purchased in Italy during your recent vacation to that country, and which cost you many hours of pay, can also be an object of special significance—assuming, of course, that you aren't the kind of person who buys and discards expensive items like this at whim.

The objects of special significance in my own life might appear strange to some people, but they are incredibly precious to me: the Ipod that has my entire music collection on it, my hard covered editions of Jane Austin's novels, the dozens of photo albums that I've collected through the years and which contain all of my family pictures. You might think that these sorts of things aren't worth investing so much emotion over, but that's the crazy thing about special somethings: one person's special something could literally be another's crummy piece of garbage, and visa versa.

Your Special Somethings

So what are the special somethings in your own life? Take a few moments to think about those objects in your possession that the absence of which would affect you emotionally and which would diminish the quality of your life. To help you with this process, let's do the following exercise:

Exercise: The Hurricane

Imagine that your house and everything you possess was being threatened by a rapidly approaching hurricane. To help you and your family survive, your car needs to be filled mostly with food and water. You have enough room to take five—and only five— personal items with you. You don't have to worry about family members or pets, because they have been accounted for. You have only ten minutes to make your decision before your family's car leaves. So what specific things, out of all the things you possess, would you take with you?

1. Laptop = contains 100's photos

2. ceramic santa music box plays White christmas was my mom's

3. family jewelry

4. Charlie Brown nativity music box

5. Family China/silver

For some people, this exercise is impossibly difficult, because they think that they have potentially dozens of special somethings. But this actually cheapens the meaning of the term. The hurricane exercise is meant to force you to make decisions about which objects you possess are truly meaningful to you. If you find it impossible to make a decision because you think that everything in your home is a special something, then you may want to think about whether or not you have a serious addiction to stuff.

Other people have the opposite problem. They are so uninterested in material things that they find it difficult even to think about five items that they would salvage after the important people in their lives have been taken care of. Although there are definitely people who are not interested at all in material things—we usually refer to them as monks—most of us are in fact attached to a few things in our lives. These may not be the most obvious things, so you might have to think carefully about which objects in your life you come back to again and again for pleasure, utility, or inspiration. If you think carefully about it, odds are that you can find five items in your possession to which you have at least some sort of emotional attachment.

Special Somewheres

Our special somethings are not limited solely to the objects in our possession. We can bestow affection and fondness upon places as well. A place is simply a portion of space occupied by people and/or things. The physical space that comprises a place can be confined (a narrow hallway) or vast (the Grand Canyon); it can be indoors (the kitchen) or outdoors (the local park); it can be completely private (your bedroom) or very public (a shopping mall); it can be incredibly ugly (the bathroom of an inner city bus station) or exquisitely beautiful (Notre Dame Cathedral).

Most places we typically visit don't necessarily have special significance. The supermarket we frequent to buy our food or streets we walk down on our way to work are places, but we don't necessarily feel any sort of fondness or affection for them. They're just space that we pass through to accomplish the business of life and nothing more.

So what exactly is a special somewhere? Like any other sort of important thing in your life, a special somewhere is a place that you have imbued with affection and fondness and which therefore has a greater significance for your life than most other places. Special somewheres are those spots that you return to again and again, either physically or in your mind. They are places that bring you joy when you are able to go to them and sadness when you are away from them for too long. They are also places that, for one reason or another, have helped to shape the person that you have become.

For some people, a special somewhere can be an entire city or particular street within that city; for others it might be a place of natural beauty far removed from all vestiges of civilization. It could be a favorite restaurant, bookstore, or coffee shop that you continually frequent, or it could be a place that you've only been to once, but which made a deep and lasting impression upon you. Special somewheres don't have to be anywhere very dramatic: one's own bedroom, kitchen, or backyard can be one of the most important places in a person's life, particularly if that person is a bit of a homebody.

Now let's see where your special somewheres are:

Exercise: The Places I Remember

Think about those places that you find yourself returning to again and again. The places in your life that have helped to define who you are as a human being, because they are so significant to you. So what are these places?

1. Coopers Town
2. Jackai Reillys
3. My house/home
4. Any where c my family
5.

Once again, you may have had trouble limiting your special somewheres to only five, if you're a natural born explorer. Or you might have had trouble getting beyond your own house.

Hopefully, however, you've identified at least five somewheres to go along with the five somethings that you've also identified. We'll be using your list in just a little bit to help you develop the skill of concentrated awareness, so it's important to take the time to identify both the significant things and places in your life, before you go on any further.

Express Yourself

4.1. Thing I Love. Choose one object that you listed as a special something on the Hurricane exercise. If you have this item, put it in front of you and examine it carefully, almost as though you were investigating an object from another planet. Now write about that object in as much detail as possible. If you prefer, you can write about it in the form of a poem or tell a story associated with that object.

4.2. Favorites. Do you have a favorite food, book, movie, TV show, album or song? If so, choose one of these to write about and reflect upon what it is about this thing that makes you appreciate it so much.

4.3. A Family Heirloom. Most families have at least one kind of heirloom—something precious that has been passed down from one generation to the next. It could be a piece of jewelry or furniture, a work of art, antique photos, or even old letters. Heirlooms don't necessarily have to be valuable, but they do need to be valued. If there is an heirloom in your family that you've always admired and wanted to possess, describe what it is and what its significance is for you.

4.4. Souvenir. Find some souvenir that you kept through the years from a family vacation, a trip, a relationship, etc. Describe this object in detail and the events surrounding your acquisition of the souvenir.

4.5. The Thing I Absolutely Hate. The flipside of love is hate. You probably possess one or two items that you absolutely loathe, but were forced to keep for one reason or another. You can also write about something that you are forced to use regularly and hate, even if you don't own it. Write about this object in as much detail as possible.

4.6. The Place I Love. The following exercise comes from Natalie Golberg's *Writing Down the Bones*: "Visualize a place that you really love, be there, see the details. Now write about it. It could be a corner of your bedroom, an old tree you sat under one whole summer, a table at McDonald's in your neighborhood, a place by the river. What colors are there, sounds, smells? When someone else reads it, she should know what it is like to be there. She should feel how you love it, not by your saying you love it, but by your handling of the detail." (23).

4.7. In My Room. No matter how cramped or messy it might be, or who you have to share it with, your bedroom is typically a place of special signifiance, mainly because you spend so much time there and have so many memories (good and bad) associated with it. This exercise has been adapted from one found in Kathleen Adam's *Journal to the Self* (82-82). Investigate your bedroom at home as though you were a private detective trying to figure out what sort of person lives in the room. Describe that person based solely upon the evidence found in the room.   If you have your own apartment or house, you can broaden your focus.

4.8.   The Place I Absolutely Hate. The flipside of the place you love. Describe this place thoroughly so we know what it is that you hate about this place.

4.9. Longings. Sometimes our sense of personal identity is shaped more by our longings than by what we actually possess. Are there any things you don't have yet that you've always dreamed about owning? Any places that you haven't been to where you've always wanted to go? What are they? How do you think these desires might help shape your sense of identity?

Scratching
The Surface

5

Who Am I?

W ho am I? This is probably the ultimate philosophical question.
It has been the problem that great thinkers have struggled with
since the time of Socrates, the father of Western Philosophy,
and has preoccupied philosophers ever since. The question gets to the
heart of what it means to be a human being in general, but also a specific
human being with his or her own unique identity.

We can interpret the question in a number of different ways: What
does it mean to be a human being? Or what does it mean to be this concrete
individual, inhabiting this particular body, living at this specific time in
history? If we want to get really abstract, we could even ask, what is
the being of the particular being that I am? What is my essence, in other
words?

Pretty heady stuff, isn't it?

If you were asked to describe who you are, there are probably a
million things that you could say about yourself that reflect your unique
nature as a human being. Some verbose individuals could probably fill a
book just answering this question. And it is undoubtedly true that each
individual's attempt to answer the question, "Who am I?" will be at least
slightly different in numerous ways from everyone else's answers to this
question.

So who are you, anyway?

I am What I Appear to Be: The Persona

One of the founders of modern psychology, Carl Jung, attempted to answer just this question by focusing on that aspect of human personality that he calls the "persona." Jung describes the persona as a kind of mask that people put on that serves two purposes: First, it presents an image of ourselves to the world, an image that reflects the way we would like to be perceived. Second, it serves to conceal the kind of person we actually are.

If you are like most people, you probably don several different masks depending upon the audience with whom you are interacting. For your parents, you might be "the good little boy" or "cute little girl" (even if you are over 50). For your friends, you might be "the class clown" or the "wild rebel." As you get older and take on more responsibility, you might put on the mask of "the company man" or "concerned citizen."

In fact, as you get older, the masks you wear will probably become even more solidly fixed. You will become "a teacher," "a doctor," "a mother," "a Republican," "an atheist"...or however else you might choose to describe yourself based upon the roles that you've selected in life. There might even come a time when the mask becomes totally and completely who you are and nothing else remains.

There is nothing inherently wrong with wearing masks. Some psychologists believe that such wearing masks at times helps human beings get along with one another more easily. The problem with identifying yourself with a persona is that it really isn't who you actually are. It is a subterfuge, a fiction that you create about yourself to prevent other people from seeing you as you actually are.

But why would anyone want to conceal his or her true identity from the rest of the world? The answer is that the vast majority of people are often so insecure about their authentic selves that they are terrified that if others know who they really are, they will reject them. In some ways, it's far easier to live a fiction—to pretend to be someone other than who we actually are—than to risk the horrible possibility of being scorned. So we create the mask. And then when others don't like what they see, it is the mask that they are rejecting, so it's not quite as painful.

The various masks we wear both reveal as well as conceal. But what exactly do they serve to reveal and what do they attempt to conceal?

What is Revealed?

As I've mentioned, different people will answer the question "Who Am I?" in a wide variety of ways. Here's the response of Pam Pachedly, a typical college freshman:

Who Am I?
(Part 1)
by Pam Pachedly

I am an 18 year old girl from Valley Stream, NY. I am 5'9", have light brown hair and blue eyes. I am about average weight for my height although I could probably stand to lose a few pounds. I have a tattoo on my back that is based upon an image I saw in a magazine. It is a rose entangled in thorns. I guess that sums me up pretty well.

Most people would describe me as a fairly outgoing person who loves to laugh and have a good time. I enjoy being with people and keeping busy with work and activities (soccer, movies, and get-togethers with friends especially). I find it difficult to deal with down-time. When I am home alone with nothing to do, it is very difficult for me. I guess that's why I try to keep as busy as possible. During down-time I am almost always on my cell phone, calling or texting friends. I guess that I just like to keep connected.

The thing that I hate more than anything else in life is phoniness. As much as possible, I try to be sincere about the way I feel, and I hate it when people say one thing and act a completely different way. I also have no time for the shallow kinds of activities that kids my own age usually engage in—drinking, smoking, and getting high especially. I think that if you can't find any meaning out of life without messing up your mind with shit, you probably should just give it up right now.

Notice the way that Pam initially went about answering the question, "Who am I?" focused primarily on three things: her physical characteristics (18, female, brown hair, blue eyes, average weight, tattoo), her personality (outgoing, fun-loving, a bit manic, extroverted), and her attitudes and beliefs (likes sincerity and hates phoniness, dislikes shallow recreational pursuits, especially those involving mind-altering substances).

Pam's reponse to the question, "Who am I?" is fairly typical. The three aspects of her identity that she focuses on—appearance, personality, and attitudes—are usually the first things young people try to "manage" when presenting themselves to others. Although there are numerous other masks that we put on for others, these three can be said to form the core dimension of our perrsonas. They represent the "first face" we present to the world in our attempt to define who we are as human beings.

What is Concealed?

If the persona is adopted by individuals to reveal certain carefully selected aspects of themselves to the world, it also serves to disguise those aspects of our identity which we'd rather not let others see.   Jung uses the metaphor of the "mirror" to describe the process whereby one gets beyond the superficial aspects of the persona and begins to look at the real person who lives behind the mask:

> Whoever looks into the mirror of the water will see first of all his own face. Whoever goes to himself risks a confrontation with himself. The mirror does not flatter, it faithfully shows whatever looks into it; namely the face we never show to the world because we cover it with the persona, the mask of the actor. But the mirror lies behind the mask and shows the true face (*Collected Works*, Vol. 9, 43).

But what exactly is it that we are trying to conceal when we adopt a particular persona? For one thing, there is one's real physical self, which more often than not is less appealing than we would like it to be. Commercials and advertisements have given us an ideal of what it means to be attractive and healthy that usually is unattainable by the average person. If Brad Pitt and Angelina Jolie are the norm for what we should all look like, then we are all bound to fall short to one degree or another.

Instead of accepting the fact that they are less than physically perfect, many people spend countless hours attempting to disguise who they really are with makeup and perfume, tanning, obsessive dieting, hair coloring, and, in extreme cases, through excessive use of plastic surgery. They literally begin to wear a mask that covers up the very blemishes, disfigurations, and bodily imperfections that actually make them unique individuals.

When he was having his portrait painted, Oliver Cromwell, a big-wig in Reformation England, noticed that the portrait artist had left off an unsightly mole on his face. Most important people would have been very happy to have been painted in a more flattering light for posterity. But not Cromwell. "Paint me as I am, wart and all," he told the artist.

How many people do you know who have the courage to look at themselves in the mirror first thing in the morning and accept what they see without shame or self-reproach? That sort of honesty is even more rare in our own times than it was in Cromwell's.   Most people would rather do just about anything else than stare at their naked selves in the mirror and confront their own fabulous imperfections. As Jung points out, the mirror does not flatter. It reflects who we actually are with harsh, unfeeling honesty.

The various masks we wear also are an attempt to cover up who we are internally. As we will discuss in greater detail later on, most human beings, to one degree or another, are rather dysfunctional. With the exception of a few extraordinary individuals—the Buddha, Jesus Christ, and Gandhi come to mind—most of us are bundles of neuroses, insecurities, obsessions, harmful habits, and addictive tendencies.

We definitely don't want others to see us as we actually are, because we believe that if they see through the mask we create for ourselves, we doubt that they could ever really like us. In a poem from his deeply disturbing collection, *See a Grown Man Cry, Now Watch Him Die*, Henry Rollins observes that human beings frequently create fictional selves that are happy, secure, well-adjusted, and always smiling all the time through life's adversities.

> I'm looking at a picture of myself
> In the picture I'm smiling
> I know better than that
> I wear a mask
> On the outside that's what they see
> I don't want to talk about the rest of it
> I don't want them to ask about me
> I don't want them to know me
> I can put a magnifying glass on myself
> I dissect, I look closely, too closely
> I fall silently into myself
> Self perpetuated, self involved, self destroyed
> I don't want for interaction with others
> That kind of perspective is not true
> It's true to life, not true to me
> Time to go outside
> Where's the mask

We do the same things with our attitudes and beliefs: we sanitize them to make them more appealing to others. We might have bigoted, sexist, xenophobic tendencies, but we are smart enough not to reveal these openly. So instead, we become paragons of political correctness, parading sterile, conformist beliefs aimed at winning the approval of the smart set. In the end, more of who we actually are becomes concealed than revealed. We turn ourselves into complete fictions because we are afraid of being rejected by those who won't accept us for who we are.

Exercise: My Masks

What are some of the masks that you often find yourself wearing in your own life:

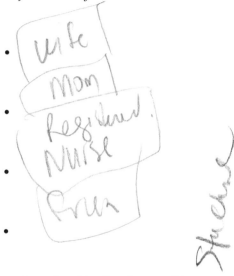

-
-
-
-

Lowering the Mask...Just a Bit

The irony is that by continually presenting a fictitious presence to the world, we all but guarantee that we will be loved, not for who we actually are, but for the fictitious mask we wear. Then our worst will actually have been realized: there truly is nothing about us that is intrinsically worthwhile; we become worthwhile only when we maintain the fiction of being other than who we actually are.

We also lose that which actually makes us unique and interesting to others. After all, it is our flaws, weaknesses, and gross imperfections that make us so damned fascinating. There never was, and never will be a novel written or a film made about a perfect individual, because perfection is just plain boring.

There is something liberating about stripping away the various masks that we wear and allowing our true selves to shine through. It takes a great deal of courage to do this, and certainly not everyone is capable of such personal transparency. But there are incredible rewards awaiting those who make the effort.

For Reflection

1. If you were to ask acquaintainces of yours (not good friends or family members) who they would say you are, how do you think they would respond?

   Baker
   Nurse

2. How do you think close friends or family members would answer this question?

   good wife/mom
   Serious but silly at times

3. Now how would you answer this same question?

   wife mom nurse
   care about family friends PJs

4. Are the answers to questions 1-3 basically the same or do they differ substantially? What do you think this might indicate about your own persona?

   very simple

Express Yourself

5.1 Who Am I? We've seen that this is not a very easy question to answer. Hopefully you have thought about this question suffiicently now that you can tackle it head on. T,ry to avoid answering this question in a strictly literal fashion ("I'm a 19 year old girl from Valley Stream"), but rather attempt to be a bit more imaginative about it.

If you are feeling overwhelmed by the idea of attempting this piece, you might begin by writing the words "I am" on the top of a blank sheet of paper and then writing down as many descriptive phrases as you can that capture who you are as an individual. The more descriptive phrases you put down on your sheet, the easier it will be to write this piece.

Once you have enough ideas jottted down, you need to decide what form your "Who Am I?" piece should take. Here are just a few possibilities:

5.1.1. Write it as a piece of straightforward prose. Just be as descriptive as you possibly can.

5.1.2. If you feel whimsical, you can write a humorous, or you can take an ironical tone to the whole idea of attempting to define yourself at all.

5.1.3. If you feel like taking a more creative approach, you can write this piece as a long poem, a dialogue, or even a story.

5.1.4. If you feel like being abstract about it, try writing a philosophical piece, exploring the question of human identity in an abstract way.

5.1.5. If you feel annoyed at having to limit your identity at all, you can write a piece rejecting the whole idea of attemtping to write a "Who Am I" piece.

The really important thing to keep in mind is that there is absolutely no right or wrong way to approach this question.

5.2. That's Not Who I Am! Very often in life people form an impression of you that is difficult to shake. If you are perceived as being a very different person from who you actual think you are, then write about this dichotomy, what you think the reason for it is, and how you feel about it .

5.3. What's My Mask? We have seen that people put on all different kinds of masks to try to shape the image that others have of them or to cover up aspects of their own identities that they would rather not have people see. Choose one of the masks that you typically put on for the benefit of others. Explore how it is you chose to adopt this mask, what purpose wearing it serves you, and what the consequences would be for removing this mask.

5.4. My Ultimate Desire. Quite often an individual's identity is shaped by what he or she desires most in life. What is one of your own ultimate desires in life. Your ultimate desire can be financial, intellectual, spiritual, or interpersonal; it can be incredibly profound or farily frivilous; it can also be relatively easy to attain or virtually impossible. If you are having touble identifying an ultimate goal, try thinking about what you usually obsess over most, what makes your soul hungry, or what inspires intense envy when you see it attained in someone else's life.

5.5. Life Goals. Similar to desires, life goals can often tell quite a lot about how you perceive yourself. Try reflecting on one of these questions: Where do you see yourself 20 years from now? What will you be doing? Who will you be doing it with? What will your life be like? Remember, life goals are a kind of personal fantasy, so feel free to be impractical or unrealistic if you want.

6

Appearance

The *persona*, we have seen, is a kind of mask that we all wear; it's the public face that we present to the world that portrays us in the specific sort of light in which we would like to be seen. It's not our most authentic self, but a kind of illusion that we fabricate—with greater or lesser skill—to try to win the approval of others.

The most basic aspect of an individual's persona pertains to his or her appearance. Indeed, the first thing we often notice about someone is what he or she looks like. If you meet someone at a party, for example, and are asked by someone else what they are like, you are liable to begin by saying something along the lines of, "Well, he's tall, pretty thin, and has a balding head"—all attributes related to appearance. If you had time, you'd eventually go on to discuss this individual's personality and opinions, but that would typically come after a detailed description of his physical appearance.

Using another Latin term, we can refer to that aspect of the persona that involves appearance as the "*imago*." The term literally means image or reflection, although when applied to the persona, it refers to an idealized image of a person. It's this idealized image that we normally seek to create in our various attempts to "manage" our appearances.

And manage we do! Most people—especially young people—expend an enormous amount of time, energy, and money insuring that they present themselves in the most flattering light possible. Even individuals who intentionally disfigure themselves with tattoos, piercings, and other sorts of bodily modifications are engaged in their own sort of image control. The same is true of those who go around in grungy clothes and look like they haven't taken a shower in two weeks. They are revealing about themselves precisely what they want others to see.

Revealing

So what is it that we want others to notice about our *imago*—our idealized image? What do you think you are you revealing about yourself by:

1. the way you dress (up or down).
2. how much of your body you choose to expose when you are dressing (or how little).
3. how much effort you spend having your hair cut just the right way.
4. how much time you spend shopping for just the right clothes, jewelry, or accessories, and how much you are willing to spend on these items.
5. how much time you spend obsessing in the mirror about how you look.
6. what sort of bodily adornments (tattoos, piercings, etc) you choose to embrace.
7. how much time you spend exercising or watching what you eat to stay in shape.
8. how much make-up you typically put on (or avoid putting on).
9. how much time you spend trying to make yourself look cool or stylish (or the opposite).

Now there certainly might be individuals who spend almost no time at all thinking about how they look. But when we consider that even Mother Teresa and Gandhi took the time to think about what kind of image they were presenting—you think it's easy to wear a sari or loin cloth just the right way?—it is evident that the vast majority of human beings are at least somewhat focused on matters of appearance.

If you haven't thought much about what kind of idealized image you are trying to present to the world, here's a little exercise for you:

Exercise: My Idealized Image

The next time you are going out for a night on the town, or have spent time dressing up for school or work, examine yourself carefully in a mirror. A full-length mirror will be best for this sort of exercise, but, if you don't have one, any mirror will do. Give yourself at least 15 minutes, so you take the time to really observe yourself.

Now, study the image in the mirror as though it belonged to a total stranger. Study it very carefully, noting as much detail about the person in the mirror as you can.

Pretend that you have to report back to a friend about what the person you are staring at in the mirror looks like (and this is a friend who likes to know everything!). How would you go about describing the person in the mirror in as objective a manner as possible? Begin by just writing down every reaction your have to the image in the mirror without attempting to censor yourself in any way.

Let's push this exercise one step further and do a little psychoanalysis: What sort of image would you say the person in the mirror is trying to present to the world? What message is being sent by the way he or she dresses or is made up? Based solely upon the image presented in the mirror, does this seem like a person who is comfortable with the way he or she looks or not? Finally, if you have to use one adjective to capture the "look" of the person in the mirror for your friend, what would this word be?

How difficult was it for you to do this exercise? If you are like most people, the idea of studying yourself almost like a object of scientific investigation was probably somewhat uncomfortable. Most of us *look* at ourselves every day in the mirror, but we rarely spend the time to *see* the face starting back at us.

Concealing

Our exercise doesn't end here. You may recall that the various masks we wear that create our *persona* serve two distinct purposes—they reveal that which we want others to notice about ourselves, but they also conceal. So when it comes to the idealized physical image that we present to the world, the manner in which we dress, style our hair, or put on makeup also serves to conceal things about ourselves that we don't want others to notice. It's this concealing aspect of the *persona* that we want to focus on now:

Exercise: Examining The Stranger

Take five more minutes to stare at the image in the mirror as though it belonged to a stranger. This time, however, the stranger is clearly someone who has something to hide about him or herself, and you are an investigative reporter who has nothing to go on but this mysterious stranger's physical appearance. What is being concealed by the image that this person presents to you may not be quite as evident as what he or she is trying to reveal, so take some time to study the reflection in the mirror carefully. Based solely upon your observations of the image presented in the mirror, what exactly do you think the mysterious stranger is trying to hide from the rest of us?

The natural inclination of most people is simply to assume that who they are is exactly as they appear to the world, but this is very often not the case. When it comes to appearance, there are very few people who are deliriously happy about how their look (This is true even for the most glamorous models and film stars). "Make-up" really should be called "cover-up" since most people use it either to enhance their attractive features or to disguise their less desirable physical traits (e.g., a nose that is a bit too large, a slightly weak chin, eyes that are a tad too close together). The same is true for the clothes we wear, our accessories, and hair styles....The element of concealment in the idealized image that we present is always lurking as a secondary motive in our attempts at image control.

Stripping Away the Mask

Although it is quite normal for people to adopt a physical persona, we also know that authentic existence ultimately demands that at some point we strip away the mask we wear so that others will come to know us for who we really are. In terms of physical appearance, authenticity usually comes unwillingly for most people at that point in their lives—usually in middle age—when no amount of exercise, diet, cosmetic surgery, or prayer can hide any longer the effects of aging. Even those middle-aged movie stars who spend a fortune on face lifts, tummy tucks, and implants ultimately are forced eventually to realize that their efforts to stop the sands of time from slipping away are doomed to failure. Some middle aged and older people accept this fact gracefully and come to embrace their bodies as friends; others resist the realities of aging as long as possible, often becoming gross caricatures of their former selves.

Although *imago* usually refers to an idealized physical image of the self that we create for the world, there is another kind of self-image that is more authentic, because it more accurately reflects the reality of who we are as individuals. We can refer to this as the *imago naturalis*—the natural image of the physical self. To the extent that we can embrace this *imago naturalis*, to that extent will we probably be happier with who we are as individual human beings with all the flaws and physical limitations that every human being possesses. To be able to say, "This is who I am... warts and all" and be content with that reality is undoubted an enormous advantage as we pass through life.

With this in mind, let's try another exercise—this one considerably more difficult than the last. Using the same mirror with which you explored your idealized image, this time you will be investigating your natural image, and trying, as best you can, to come to terms with it. This is not an easy exercise for most people, so if you feel overly conflicted about it, just skip it for now and come back to it at some later point when you feel more comfortable about trying it.

Exercise: My Natural Image

This exercise should be done before you have engaged in any attempts at image control. Do it as soon as you wake up in the morning or right after you get out of the shower. Definitely do it before you put on any make-up or put a brush to your hair. You can attempt this exercise in whatever you normally wear to bed (if you are doing it first thing in the morning), wrapped in a towel (if you are doing it after a shower), in your underwear, or, if you feel really courageous, in your "birthday suit" (Just be sure that your grandmother is not around when you do it!).

Once again spend at least 15 minutes staring intensely at the image in the mirror as though it belonged to a complete stranger. Try to notice everything you can about this person's natural physical image. Start from the tip of your head and work your way down as far as the mirror will allow. How do you feel now about the person you are examining in the mirror? You shouldn't feel self-conscious or insecure, because, remember, this is not you....It's some total stranger.

The stranger is hiding nothing from you. The mask has been unveiled and you are seeing the stranger's natural image devoid of most of the artifices that he or she uses to obscure it. Once again describe what you see in as objective a way as possible, noting everything you find interesting, attractive, and unappealing about the person in the mirror. Whenever you start to feel overly critical, remind yourself again and again that you are observing a total stranger.

This exercise can be a deeply disturbing one for those who possess a highly self-critical body image (which is most of us). Keeping to the idea that the image in the mirror belongs to a stranger is meant to help soften some of this internal criticism. Actually, if you think about it objectively, most human beings are neither runway model gorgeous or totally repulsive. Even the most attractive models have blemishes that need to be covered over with makeup and touched up for magazine spreads. And even the most humble-looking individual has physical traits that are appealing if he or she can just get beyond excessive self-criticism.

We are, in short, who we are, and that should be fine in and of itself. Many people, however, spend their entire lives feeling self-consciousness, unhappiness, and even revulsion about their appearances. The slight spare tire or the tiny mole on the face that no one probably even notices becomes a constant reminder of their gross imperfection. To get beyond this kind of irrational self-criticism, one needs to make peace with his or her *imago naturalis,* and to embrace it as a dear friend. This, of course, is an extremely difficult thing to do successfully, and probably requires a lifetime of effort. So if you plan to succeed at all with this project, you'd better start as soon as possible!

Bits and Pieces

What we have been doing in the above exercise is to use the practice of mindful awareness to examine our natural image and to try to attain some degree of objectivity about it. But to really come to terms with who we are as physical beings, we need to dig even deeper. If we were studying a flower—as Keisha did in Chapter 3—it would not be enough to take in the whole flower. We might start with the whole, but a serious examination would lead us to the parts as well—the petals, the stems, the stamen, and even the little wafts of pollen that have fallen on the leaves. We would come to see that the whole of any thing is made up of numerous parts, each of which is thoroughly fascinating in its own way.

But what about the parts that make up the whole that is YOU? Have you ever taken the time to notice just how incredible each and every facet of your physical being actually is? Let's take one simple example: your left hand. When was the last time that you ever actually looked carefully at your hand? If you did, you'd notice all sorts of really interesting things about it: the veins running across the top, the shininess of the nails, the infinite number of wrinkles and creases that expand and contract as you move your hand, the way each digit moves gracefully (and automatically) when your mind instructs it to, and of course, the life lines on your palm that fortune tellers love to read. It doesn't matter whether this hand is bony or plump, withered or smooth as a babies', because it is a thing of such variety and complexity that it is automatically a fascinating and beautiful object of exploration.

This is true no matter how you feel about your hand (self-conscious or not) and it is true as well about every single part of your anatomy. If you take the time to examine the bits and pieces that make up the whole that is you, and you do so with some degree of objectivity, you really can't help but be enthralled. Let's try this out with one last exercise:

Exercise: Just a Bit

You can do this exercise by spending at least ten minutes staring at one specific part of your anatomy. If this part is not directly visible by looking at it (your back, for example), you may need to use a mirror to look at it.

You can pick any part of yourself to focus in on: eyes, nose, lips, neck, hands, feet, stomach, legs, etc. If you feel the old self-critic coming out, pick a part that you feel fairly positive about; if you feel more courageous, pick a part that you've always felt self-conscious about. Now explore that part once again as though it belonged to someone other than yourself. Move it, stretch it, bend it (if you can). Try to notice the complexity and variety of the body part you are examining: the texture and color of the skin around it, the way muscles and bones interact, the scars or blemishes on it.

Now, if this was the body part of a total stranger, how would you go about describing it? Pretend that the body part you've chosen is going on sale in a body parts catalogue (I know that this is silly, but just go with it). How would you describe this part to a prospective customer? Don't settle for a shallow description. Go in deep and talk about as many unique features as possible of this body part.

You don't have to stop with one part of your anatomy. Explore them all, one by one. Start from the top of your head and work your way downward to your toes....if you dare. And any time you start to get self-critical about any particular body part, just step back and treat this part with the objectivity and compassion it deserves. If you do this enough, you may start to realize that things about your appearance that you thought were unappealing are actually quite wonderful if viewed from the right perspective.

A Final Word on Appearance

By now you are probably sick and tired of staring at yourself in the mirror. The exercises in this chapter, however, are important because, for better or for worse, you are not simply a mind that happens to be trapped in a body (a view that has sarcastically been referred to by philosophers as "the ghost in the machine" approach to human identity). You *are* a flesh and blood being. The image that stares back at you from the mirror in the morning or when you get out of the shower *is* the real you. It's the real you, not despite its flaws and imperfections, but precisely because of them. Every pimple and scar on your body helps tell the tale that is you, and therefore should be embraced as a dear friend.

This is not to say that it's possible or even completely desirable to get rid of the *imago*—the idealized image of yourself that you create as part of your persona management process. That well-manicured, delightfully coiffed, exquisitely dressed version of yourself that you put on for the world is also—for better or for worse—the real you. It helps you get nice jobs, make friends, and attract lovers. Just don't think that this idealized representation is the only you or that it can last forever. Use the mask as you need to, but also be prepared to discard it when it no longer serves its purpose.

For Reflection

1. How do you feel about your appearance? Are you self-conscious or accepting about the way you look? If you are self-conscious, what exactly do you think you are self-concious about?

2. What aspect of your appearance are you most happy with? If you could change one thing about your appearance, what would it be?

3. How comfortable or uncomfortable was it for you to do some of the exercises in this chapter? Which one did you have the most trouble with? Why do you think that is?

Express Yourself

6.1. My Idealized Self. After doing the "My Idealized Self" exercise in this chapter, write a detailed description of the image that is portrayed in the mirror. If you prefer you can create a story about the person in the mirror or write a poem about him/her.

6.2. Let's Face it. Stare at your face in the mirror intensely for at least five minutes acting as though you were staring at a total stranger's face. Note every pimple, every defect, every scar, every amazing feature that you see in the mirror. Now write about that face as descriptively (and as honestly) as possible.

6.3. The Naked Truth. Go back to the "My Natural Image" exercise from earlier in this chapter and write about the results of this exercise. The key is to try to describe your features objectively and dispassionately—as though they belong to a stranger—noting those features of your physical being that are truly unique to you. Use your observations to write a purely descriptive essay or, if you feel more inspired, a poem or story.

6.4. Bits and Pieces. For this exercise, we are going to move away from the whole and look at specific details of your physical appearance.
   6.4.1. Any Old Piece of Me. Take one part of your body that you are able to examine in close detail (your eyes, hands, feet, legs, back, neck, etc). Describe that body part in as much detail as you can. If there are any interesting stories associated with that body part, tell them. If you feel inclined to write a poem about that part, write it.
   6.4.2. The Part I Hate. Everyone has some aspect of his or her physical appearance that he or she is self-concious about. It could be a big nose, a weak chin, flabby belly, or receding hairline. Describe this part of your body in as much detail and possible and then explore your feelings about it.

6.5. Scar Stories. G. Lynn Nelson writes, "Scar stories seem to come easily to us—from childhood to old age, people like to tell stories about their wounds, their operations, their accidents. And Nietzsche tells us that we must 'come to love our scars.' This exploration involves looking at your physical scars, your literal wounds, and telling the stories that come with them and need to be told." Pick one of the scars you have on your body and describe how you received it and what you remember about it (110).

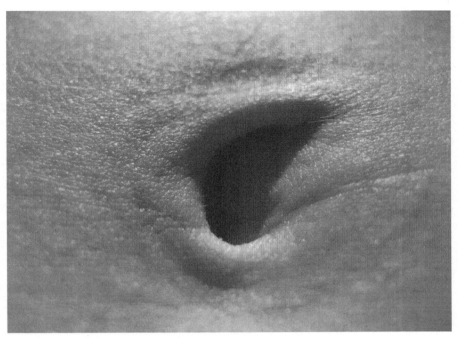

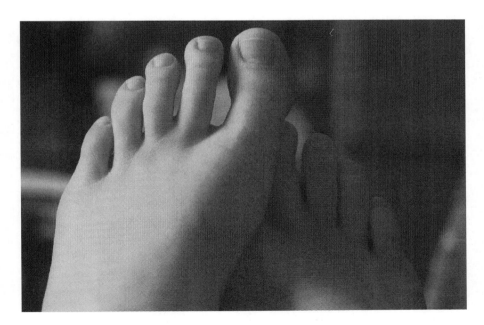

7

Personality

Having explored your physical appearance as the most obvious manifestation of your *persona*, we now move to the deeper dimension of the *persona* that is represented by the personality. The root of the word personality, as you probably realize, is, in fact, "*persona*." So personality can literally be defined as "the state of, or quality of, the *persona*." Personality, then, even more than appearance, truly represents the essence of who you are as a unique individual. It is the driving force behind most of your thoughts, motivations, and behaviors in the various life situations in which you find yourself (Ryckman, 2004).

Now, personality is an extremely complex phenomenon. Have you ever wondered how you got the particular personality you have? Clearly, there's a good part of your personality that is determined by your genetic make-up and heredity, and there's probably not much you can do about that. A significant part of your personality can also be the product of your specific upbringing, cultural influences, and your unique experiences in life. You may have more control over those aspects of your personality, but perhaps not as much as you'd like to think. So, there's a fairly sizeable part of who we are in terms of personality that seems to be given—or, to put it more bluntly, that we appear to be stuck with. Some pyschologists, in fact, believe that approximately half of our personality may be determined by forces that are essentially beyond our control.

Our personalities are also certainly not static. The personality you have right now is not the same personality you had as a child and it certainly won't be exactly the same personality you will have in old age. The fact that people often say things about one another like, "What happened to you? You used to be so _____," clearly indicates that personalities change and evolve over time. People in their middle age often lose the exhuberence and innocence they had as children, while elderly people tend to be much mellower and more easy-going then they were in their prime. Still, despite changes that take place in personality over time, there generally is a personality core that remains at least somewhat constant, or you wouldn't be the same "you" that you were in the past, or will be in the future.

Personality Types

Since ancient times, there has been a tradition of placing people into distinct catgories or types based upon their personalities. Although the science of personality categorization has gotten more sophisticated in recent years, it is still an inexact field of study at best. Most approaches fit people into rigid and distinct categories (you are either this or that). While some may find this kind of categorization too simplistic, it clearly does have its value. Understanding your personality "type" can be a first step on the road to self-discovery. Personality theories and tests have also been used successfully in recent years in individual therapy, couples counseling, and even help employees function more effectively in teams.

The Four Temperaments

One of the earliest theories of personality is known as the Four Temperaments (also known as the Four Humors). A temperament is that aspect of personality concerned with emotional reactions, their speed, and their intensity. Termperament, therefore, basically describes the "mood pattern" of a particular person.

This theory is so ancient that forms of it may go back as far as 5,000 years ago to ancient Egyptian and Mesopotamian civilizations and to the 5th century B.C. in Greece with the work of Hippocrates, the Father of Medicine. Hippocrates believed that certain [moods and behaviors] were caused by an imblance of bodily fluids (humors)—blood, yellow bile, black bile, and phlegm. Developing the insight of Hippocrates, the Greek physican, Galen, who lived in the 2nd century A.D., began looking for physiological explantions for different sorts of human behavior. Using combinations of hot and cold, dry and wet, Galen posited four temperamental categories that corresponded to each of Hippocrates' bodily humors:

- Sanguine temperaments are quick, impulsive, and have relatively short-lived reactions (hot/wet). Sanguine individuals are usually fairly extroverted, cheerful, optimistic, tend to have numerous friends, and enjoy social events.   They also have difficulty completing tasks, are usually late, tend to be forgetful, and develop passions impulsively but lose interest quickly.
- Phlegmatic temperaments have longer response time delays, but have short-lived responses (cold/wet). Fairly self-content, kind-hearted, accepting, and affectionate, phlegmatic types tend to prefer stability to change. They usually have calm and relaxed personalities, although they can also be sluggish and unemotional at times and somewhat passive-aggressive in terms of how they deal with others.
- Choleric temperaments have short response-time delays, but have responses that are sustained for a relatively long time (hot/dry). The choleric type is a doer and a leader. They tend to have quite a lot of drive, ambition, and passion, which they can sustain over time. They can also be manipulative, dominate others (especially phlegmatic types), and can be easily angered and bad-tempered.
- Melancholic temperaments have long-response time delays, have responses that are sustained at length and possibly even permanently (cold/dry). Typically interested in the arts, melancholic types tend to be creative people, who are perfectionists and tend to fixate about what they are doing to such a degree that they can forget to think about the needs of others. They also tend to obsess about the tragic state of the world, and this can lead them to have depressive personalities.

Galen believed that in a few rare individuals the qualities of hot and cold, dry and wet could be properly balanced, creating an ideal personality. Most individuals, however, have an imbalance of humors, leading one of these humors to dominate over the others.

Exercise

Look over the characteristics of the Four Temperaments listed above. Which temperament, if any, best describes you. What might be some advantages of having the sort of personality described. Some possible disadvantages?

Jungian Personality Types

A more contemporary approach to personality theory was devised by the psychologist Carl Jung and centered aound the idea of personality types. A personality type is simply a preferred way of thinking or acting that we are either born with or develop over time. Jung's theory was later developed by Katharine Cook Briggs and her daughter Isabel Briggs Myers (the Myers-Briggs Type Indicator) and popularized through the work of David Keirsey (The Keirsey Temperament Sorter).

What all these theories have in common is that they divide personality traits into four pairs or dichotomies:

- Introversion (I) vs. Extraversion (E)

    The term introvert in Jungian psychology simply means "inward turning," and extraversion means "outward-turning." The introvert's orientation is directed inward towards concepts and ideas, the extravert's is directed outward towards people and objects. Those who are introverts derive their energy from time spent alone and from the inner world of thoughts, ideas, and reflections. After spending significant time in the company of others, the introvert will typically need to retreat to a more private setting to "recharge his batteries." Extroverts derive energy from contact with others, and rarely feel drained from excessive interaction from the outside world.

- Sensing (S) vs. Intuition (N)

    Jung understood sensing and intuition as information-gathering or perceiving functions of the personality. These two describe how information is understood and interpreted. Sensors prefer to work with clear, tangible, and concrete data, or information that is gathered by the five senses. They are mainly in the facts, and tend to distrust hunches. Intuitors prefer abstract, conceptual information and often are interested in future possibilities than in concrete realities. They also tend to trust flashes of insight that surface from their unconscious minds.

- Thinking (T) vs. Feeling (F)

    Jung described thinking and feeling as decision-making functions of the personality. It's what we do with the information that we gathered through the process of sensing or intuition. Thinkers make decisions in a logical and analytical manner. Feelers, on the other hand, base their decisions upon emotions and use empathy to take into consideration the overall impact of decisions upon others.

- Judgment (J) vs. Perception (P)

   Adding an extra category to Jung's personality typology, Myers and Briggs maintained that people also have a preference for either judging or perceiving when relating to the outside world. Judgers tend to "have matters settled" and to prefer closure in their projects and activities. They also tend to stick closely to schedules and meet deadlines. Perceivers, on the other hand, tend to prefer to keep things open-ended, view schedules as being flexible, and have a more difficult time meeting deadlines.

Based upon the possible combinations of each of the pairs described above, we are left with 16 possible personality types. After completing a simple personality test, a person is then given a four letter designation, depending upon their specific personality type. An INFJ, for example would be someone whose personality is introverted (I), intuiting (N), feeling (F), and judging (J). No particular combination is better or worse than any other. The point is to try to discover what your own personality type is and then to use this information to guide you in your life decisions.

What I've included above is simply a summary of the different Jungian personality types. To see how your own personality fits, you can take one of the many Jungian personality tests available online. The best place to start is at humanmetrics.com, which has a free—though basic—Jungian Typology Test that can provide you with some useful information on your particular personality type. If you want to spend a bit more time studying your personality type, you can check out David Keirsey's popular book, *Please Understand Me,* from the library, and take the test included in that book. Keirsey's book—and the follow-up volume, *Please Understand Me II*—provides a wealth of information on each of the types listed above.

Exercise

Take the Jungian Typology Test on humanmetrics.com or the more involved one included in Keirsey's book. What was your own personality type? What did you discover about yourself based upon the information provided about your specific type?

The "Mask" of Personality

We've seen that when it comes to personality, a large part of who we are is determined by heredity or environment. However, there's also part of our personality that is shaped consciously by human beings in their on-going attempts at personality management. Most human beings, we know, do all they can to present an image of themselves to the word that represents how they would like to be perceived—or at least how they think they would like to be perceived. Just as we control the physical aspects of our persona through appearance management, we do the same thing with our personalities. We shape and adjust them to meet the expectations that the world has about us.

For example, 20 year old Cassie, a junior in college, describes her own personality in the following way:

> *I guess you could say that I'm basically a shy person who loves to hang out in my own room listening to music or reading a book. My bedroom is my personal sanctuary. I go there when I need to de-stress from life and get away from it all. There's something nice about being able to wrap yourself up in the cocoon of your bed, turn on some Beyonce (she's my favorite!), and just forget about everything.*
>
> *That's not to say that I'm a loner, or anything like that. I have tons of great friends who I hang out with all the time. I spend most of my weekends with them going to clubs to dance and meet guys. If you asked any of my friends, they'd probably say that I'm a blast when we go out to party. It's just that there's a side of me that needs escape from all that and be by myself for a while. I don't think there's anything wrong with that.*

From her description, it's obvious that Cassie is basically an introvert at heart. She derives much of her energy from being on her own, in the "sanctuary" of her bedroom. Her friends, however, expect her to join them on their weekend outing to dance clubs and to be outgoing and fun-loving while they are out. Cassie, in turn, feels compelled to accommodate them and adjusts her personality accordingly to become the kind of "blast" that would be popular among her college-aged companions.

Accommodations like this go on all the time in the process of persona adjustment. Someone may be wild and passionate at heart, but feels compelled to "tone it down" to function in a conservative work environment. Another may be highly emotional and sensitive, but has been taught by his uptight parents to suppress his emotions because "big boys don't cry." We make adjustments like these all the time to fit in and to succeed in life, and that's perfectly normal.

Stripping Away the Mask...Just a Bit

However, just as there is a more authentic you in terms of appearance, there is also a personality that is more naturally yours than the one you put on to appease others. Cassie, for example, is at heart an introvert, but she may not even be fully aware of this because she spends so much time managing her personality for the benefit of her friends. Although this is a natural process for most people, there also is a price we pay when we fail to understand our authentic personality type.

There really is no better or worse type than any other, and, as you read up on the different personality types, you'll quickly discover that there are advantages and disadvantages to each type. The key to living a happy and well-adjusted life is to have some understanding of your unique type and to use this information to try to develop yourself as a human being, understand what motivates you, and to grasp, as much as possible, what motivates those around you.

But you can't do any of that if you insist on never letting down the mask of personality that you've devised for yourself.

For Reflection

1. Look over the adjectives on the following pages If you had to sum up your personality using any words from the list, what would they be?

2. What adjectives from the list would people who don't know you very well (classmates, co-workers, casual acquaintances) use to describe your personality?

3. Finally, what adjectives would people who know you extremely well (family members, close friends, partners) use to describe your personality?

4. Reflect: Are the words that you've chosen for each of these questions the same or do they vary? If they vary—and again, there's nothing surprising about that—what does this have to say about the way you manage your personality for the benefit of others?

Personality Adjectives

- Accepting
- Adaptable
- Adventurous
- Aggressive
- Ambitious
- Annoying
- Arrogant
- Articulate
- Athletic
- Awkward
- Boastful
- Bold
- Bossy
- Brave
- Bright
- Busy
- Calm
- Careful
- Careless
- Caring
- Cautious
- Cheerful
- Clever
- Clumsy
- Compassionate
- Competent
- Complex
- Conceited
- Confident
- Considerate
- Cooperative
- Courageous
- Creative
- Curious
- Dainty
- Daring
- Dark
- Defiant
- Demanding

- Determined
- Devout
- Disagreeable
- Disgruntled
- Dreamer
- Eager
- Efficient
- Embarrassed
- Energetic
- Enthusiastic
- Excited
- Expert
- Fair
- Faithful
- Fancy
- Fighter
- Forgiving
- Free
- Friendly
- Frustrated
- Fun-loving
- Funny
- Generous
- Gentle
- Giving
- Gorgeous
- Gracious
- Grouchy
- Handsome
- Happy
- Hard-working
- Helpful
- Honest
- Hopeful
- Humble
- Humorous
- Imaginative
- Impulsive
- Independent

- Intelligent
- Inventive
- Jealous
- Joyful
- Judgmental
- Kind
- Knowledgeable
- Lazy
- Light-hearted
- Likeable
- Lively
- Lovable
- Loving
- Loyal
- Manipulative
- Materialistic
- Mature
- Melancholy
- Messy
- Mischievous
- Naïve
- Neat
- Nervous
- Noisy
- Obnoxious
- Opinionated
- Organized
- Outgoing
- Passive
- Patient
- Patriotic
- Perfectionist
- Personable
- Pitiful
- Plain
- Pleasant
- Pleasing
- Poor
- Popular

- Pretty
- Proper
- Proud
- Questioning
- Quiet
- Radical
- Realistic
- Rebellious
- Reflective
- Relaxed
- Reliable
- Religious
- Reserved
- Respectful
- Responsible
- Reverent
- Rich
- Rigid
- Rude
- Sad
- Sarcastic
- Self-confident
- Self-conscious
- Selfish
- Sensible
- Sensitive
- Serious
- Shy
- Silly
- Simple
- Smart
- Stable
- Strong
- Stubborn
- Studious
- Successful
- Tender
- Tense
- Thoughtful
- Thrilling
- Timid
- Tireless
- Tolerant
- Tough
- Tricky
- Trusting
- Understanding
- Unhappy
- Unique
- Unlucky
- Vain
- Warm
- Wild
- Wise
- Witty

Express Yourself

7.1. The Stranger's Personality. In the previous chapter, you were asked to describe your appearance as though you were a stranger to yourself. Now, describe your personality as though it belonged to a total stranger. Try to be as objective as possible about the strengths and weaknesses of all your dominant personality traits.

7.2. Personality Event. Very often our personalities are shaped by significant events in our lives. These events can be life-affirming (winning the 3rd grade spelling bee) or traumatic (wetting your underpants in school). Is there an event that you can recall in your own life that you think helped shape your personality? If so, write about it.

7.3. One Trait. Take one of the personality adjectives that you circled on the previous pages and explore it in relationship to your own life. How has it benefited you to have this particular trait? How has it proven to be a liability? If you prefer, you can also tell a story about a time when this trait surfaced in your life in a meaningful way, or you can write a poem about this trait.

7.4. Personal Ad. A personal ad is an attempt to distill the personality of an individual in a way that captures his or her essence for another person (usually a prospective date or partner). Of course, most people tend to spin the description that they write for a personal ad in a way that reveals what they want to show the other person and conceal what they want to hide.   The personal ad, therefore, is a perfect exercise for attempting to capture your own persona. This exercise comes from Sandy Grason's *Journalution*: "Set a timer for ten minutes and write "Personal Ad" at the top of a blank sheet of paper. Now for ten minutes, describe yourself... Who are you? How do you look to others? What are the most striking qualities of your personality? Why would someone be lucky to spend the rest of his or her life with you? What makes you unique? Who are you, really? Don't worry about the facts; you can be completely philosophical or just describe your physical qualities. Let your mind wander and your pen lead the way. Have fun!" (172).

7.5. My Failure. Sometimes failure in life shapes our personalities more profoundly than success. Describe a time that you failed miserably at something and how it affected you.

8

Attitudes and Beliefs

We have finished exploring appearance and personality as two dimensions of the persona. We are now ready to examine the final aspect of the persona—belief.

The word "belief" in Greek is *doxa*, which philosophically refers to a kind of unreflective belief or opinion that stands in contrast to knowledge (*episteme*). The philosopher Plato, for example, believed that the Truth—not my truth or your truth, but *The Truth*—is grasped by knowledge, while belief or opinion represents a kind of shadow version of the truth, one that is often illusionary and lacking certainty. Given this contrast, it would seem self-evident that a lover of the truth would be less interested in belief and more interested in cultivating knowledge for its own sake. After all, who wouldn't want to grasp *The Truth* if were possible to do so?

But can we, in fact, really grasp the truth? Stop for a moment and think about what you would consider to be absolutely, self-evidently true. If your life depended upon listing three truths that you know with utter and complete certainty, what would they be? Your truths can be about the world, your own existence within it, God, life beyond this world, or any other truth that you can claim to know with certainty.

So what would these self-evident truths be?

1.

2.

3.

Now that you've decided upon three truths that you think can be accepted with certainty, it's time to examine them to see if they really are as absolutely certain as you think they are. A certain truth would be one that was so self-evident that it would hold up to any kind of critical examination. Is that the case for the truths that you've listed?

The Whole Truth

Lets' take one proposition that most people would accept as self-evident: that the world around you exists as you perceive it. This would certainly appear to be the kind of proposition that should be able to be accepted without any sort of doubt. But is it really?

Suppose, in fact, that what you perceive to be "really real" is a kind of illusion? Haven't you ever been asleep and had a dream that seemed completely and totally real? Didn't you ever eat something delicious in one of your dreams and almost thought you could taste it? Or had a wild, erotic dream that seemed totally and completely real? How do you know you are not asleep and dreaming right now? Can you really be absolutely certain that you're not?

Or let's pretend, as the philosopher Renee Descartes did, that the world and everything you perceive in it is actually the work of some supreme evil genius out to deceive you and make you think that what is an illusion is actually real. Everything you think is true, then, would actually be a total fabrication, a complete deception. How would you go about disputing the existence of such a supreme evil genius? If he's that much of a supreme genius, you wouldn't even know that he was toying with your perception of reality, now would you?

Are you still so confident in your ability to know the Truth?

In fact, there was a group of philosophers in the ancient world known as the Skeptics who questioned whether we could know anything with certainty. Everything, no matter how true it might appear, they thought, was subject to doubt. Therefore the kind of certainty that Plato argued came with knowledge was, in fact, a delusion. At best, the Skeptics said, we might be able to say that something "appears to be the case," but we could never claim with utter conviction that something absolutely is so. If the skeptics are right, then true knowledge is ultimately impossible and all we really have are our beliefs.

Even if we don't want to go as far as the skeptics do in rejecting the whole idea of objective knowledge, the case could still be made that many of the truths that we take for granted are, in fact, much more like subjective beliefs than objective truths that can be demonstrated with certainty. Take the existence of God, which is taken as a central conviction in the faiths of Jews, Christians, and Muslims. Theists state with utter and complete certainty that there must be a God. But can the existence of a supreme being ever be demonstrated to the satisfaction of even an open-minded non-believer? Probably not. Therefore, the best we can say about whether God exists is that "I believe this to be the case." The existence of God is certainly not provable to someone who doesn't already have faith in the same way, for example, that mathematical formulas could be proven. It would appear, then, that most of the so-called absolute truths of our lives are like the conviction that there is a God: they're more a matter of belief or opinion than a matter of *The Truth*.

Your Belief System

Your personal belief system is the set of concrete precepts that guide your life and give meaning to your actions. Everyone has a belief system out of which they operate. Some people's may be more coherent or elaborate than others, but everyone has one.

We might reflect for a moment on where your beliefs come from. You might be tempted to believe that your beliefs are the result of years of deep introspection or profound thought, but, if you're like most people, this is probably not the case. In fact, many of the beliefs that people hold dear are probably not really their beliefs at all. They are probably the products of their upbringing or are influenced by the various peer groups to which they belong.

A former student of mine, for example, always used to drink lukewarm water from the tap after coming inside after exerting herself in the heat. When asked why she did this, she said that her grandmother told her that if she drank cold water on a hot day, she could get a heart attack. Upon further inquiring about whether she thought what her grandmother said was true, she replied, with a look of confusion, that she hadn't really thought about it. It was just something her grandmother always told her and she just took it for granted.

Parents, family members, and other similar authority figures in our lives help mold our belief systems when we are young. If you took the time to critically reflect upon your beliefs, you'd probably be surprised at how similar they are to those held by your mother or father. This is probably true even for those rebels who think that they've rejected all of their parent's norms and values.

As human beings enter their teenage years, however, the influence of parents on beliefs gives way to that of the peer group with whom one typically associates. If you are a computer geek, for example, and associate with other similar geeks, you will inevitably pick up some of the values of this group and share some of your own. Together you and your geek friends will be reinforcing each other's values during the process of interacting together.

Undoubtedly, there is also some element of choice in the belief systems that we choose to adopt. Like appearance and personality, belief can be a kind of mask we freely choose to wear to fit in more easily with those around us. The fact that people often change their belief systems throughout the course of their lives, also shows that some aspects of belief at least are voluntary.

But for many unreflective individuals, the beliefs of childhood that were taken on without much real choice can come to create an unassailable belief system that is rarely if ever critically examined. Rather than being in charge of their beliefs, such individuals are often controlled by imposed beliefs that have taken on the force of dogma.

What Are Your Core Beliefs?

So what exactly are those beliefs that you hold to most strongly in life? The kind of beliefs that I'm talking about now are not the flighty sort that you pick up on whim and discard willy-nilly when you realize just how idiotic they are. No, the beliefs I'm referring to now are the ones that give shape and color to your entire life; they're the beliefs that you accept almost as eternal truths because they provide your life with ultimate meaning. In fact, in answering this question, you might return to the three self-evident "truths" that you listed above as a starting point for your reflection.

If you took some time, you'd almost certainly begin to realize that you undoubtedly have strong beliefs about a wide range of topics (religious, economic, political, social, moral, cultural, philosophical, etc). Start off by thinking about issues or problems that make you passionate, angry, or inspired. Then think about where you stand on these issues. This will help to illuminate what your main beliefs are:

I believe that...

1.

2.

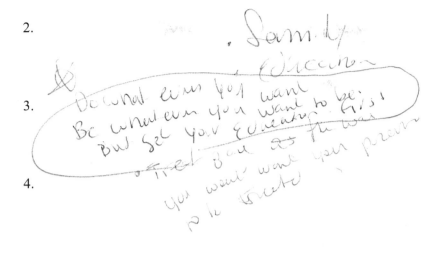

3.

4.

5.

Questioning Your Belief System

One problem with inheriting a set of beliefs is that people don't often take the time to critically question what they believe. Do the beliefs that you hold to really make sense in your present life or are they lingering vestiges from your childhood or adolescence that have outgrown their usefulness, but which you were simply too lazy or fearful to discard?

For each of the beliefs that you listed above, try assessing the following:

1. Is this belief really yours?
2. Does this really make sense?
3. Is it this belief practical?
4. Is this belief sustainable?
5. Is this belief life-enhancing?

We've seen that many people inherit belief system that they picked up unconsciously from their parents or peer groups. Sometimes these beliefssystems make sense and provide a positive and healthy framework for living out one's life; other times they represent little more than irrational dogma that gets in the way of being a truly self-actualized human being.

So what about your beliefs? Are they truly your own beliefs or did you just inherit them from others? Do they really make sense in the context of your current life? Are they practical enough to use as guides and sustainable enough that they can be held to for your entire life? Finally, do these beliefs actually serve to make your life better, happier, richer, and more fulfilled, or do are they simply dragging you down?

Express Yourself

8.1. Take a Stand. Pick some topic or issue about which you feel strongly. If you have trouble thinking of anything, reflect for a few moments on those situations which you find yourself angry, upset, or worked-up about some issue, problem, or situation. Write passionately (or at least with some conviction) about this topic.

8.2. My Beliefs. Go back to the list of your core beliefs, and choose one to examine in detail.

    8.2.1. Exploring Belief. Reflect upon what the origins of this belief might have been in your life, how this belief has served you, and how it has helped to shape your worldview.

    8.2.2. Belief in Conflict. Write about a time when one of your core beliefs came into conflict with those of another person or some instituition to which you belonged (e.g., a school, a club or organization, a political group). Describe what the cause of the conflict was and how it was ultimately resolved.

    8.2.3. Questioning Your Beliefs. Imagine what would happen if you rejected outright one of your core beliefs. What consequences would this have for your life? Explore this in writing.

    8.2.4. Belief Poem. Write a poem in celebration of one of your core beliefs.

8.3. This Has to Change! Write about one thing in our society that you think really has to change. How would you go about changing this, if you could?

8.4. Quirky Idea. Most people have some strange, controversial, or just plain bizarre ideas about something which they may be afraid to express for fear about how people will react. But quirky ideas are usual the most interesting. If you have one, write about it.

8.5. My Manifesto. One of the best ways to clarify exactly what you believe is to write a manifesto. A manifesto is nothing other than a concise statement of your beliefs. Manifestos can be personal, political, artistic, social, or cultural but should express in clear and relatively concise terms what you believe about some domain of your life and why you believe it.

Telling My Stories

9

My Stories: Present and Past

In the previous chapter, we examined the response of a typical college student to the question, "Who Am I?" The student, Pam, in her first attempt to answer this question focused on the various dimensions of her persona—appearance, personality, and attitudes. When she was asked to dig deeper she began thinking more about the significant events of her life:

Who Am I?
(Part 2)
by Pam Pachedly

I was born in 1990 in Valley Stream, Long Island and spent my first five years there. As a small child, I was a bit insecure and spent a great deal of time in the company of my mother and grandmother. My relationship with my father was always difficult and we've never really seen eye-to-eye on most issues.

As a child, I had a few friends from the neighborhood that I felt comfortable with. But mainly I spent most of my time at home, reading, watching t.v., and playing with my Barbie Dolls. I guess that you could say that I was a fairly nerdy kid.

Around the age of 13 I started to rebel and began hanging out with a crowd that was into guys and partying. Looking back on it now, I can see that I was crying out for attention, but back then I didn't know how to handle all the emotions that I was experiencing. Things got even worse during my first two years at Valley Stream High School. A lot of my friends had begun to get seriously involved in drinking, drugs, and sex, and some of them wound up getting into serious trouble because of it (jail, rehab, teen pregnancy...you know the deal). I might have ended up the same way, but during my junior year I joined the girl's soccer team at school and found a new set of friends who were more serious about life.

This year, I began my first semester of college, and so far I love it. I don't have to deal with any of the shit that was a problem in high school. Typically, I spend most of the day at classes or working out with my friends on the soccer team. Three nights a week I work at The Sports Authority to make money to help pay for school. I normally go out into the city with my friends on Friday or Saturday nights or just hang out at one of their houses. We have fun, but none of us feel the need to overdo it.

You know what they say: once a nerd, always a nerd!

Having been asked to reflect in greater depth about herself, Pam decided to write about events from her past that were significant to her—her childhood insecurities, her relationships with her mother and father, the difficulties of her adolescent years. She also decided to write about her present—how she spends her time and with whom, and what she thinks about her peers who "overdo it."

What Pam has discovered is that the question, "Who am I" can be answered by looking at significant events from her present and past life that create a coherent life narrative. Her life is filled with stories waiting to be told. Some of these stories are undoubtedly painful, many of them probably joyful, but they are all interesting because they are her stories.

What are the fascinating stories in your own life? What's going on right now in your own life that is every bit as fascinating as any story told in a novel or film? What are the curious, heartbreaking, transformational events of your past that have helped to shape the person that you have become? These are the kinds of questions that we will be asking this week.

Present Tense: What's Going On Here?

If you are like most people, you probably do an awful lot of things throughout the day. Indeed, life for most Americans is filled with so many commitments and responsibilities that most of us are kept running on overdrive all day long. By the time we go to bed at night, we have done so much, seen so much, and said so much that we often forget some of the truly amazing things that may have happened to us along the way. That is why it is so very important to stop every now and then and take notice of what exactly is going on in your life.

Of course, one might argue that the vast majority of happenings in the average person's life are so mundane that they are hardly worth conscious noting. Eating Cheerios for breakfast, getting dressed, going to the bathroom, filling up the car, after all, hardly seem worth spending so much time thinking about. Most people view these kinds of activities as the dull stuff of life—things we have to do to get by, but better done in a completely zoned-out state (That's why they invented Ipods, after all!). While there definitely is a time and a place for zoning out from life, many people seem to spend most of their lives in this state. And because of this, life passes them by without making any kind of deep impact.

What we are going to ask you to do now is to apply the method of concentrated awareness that we've been working with to the significant events of your life. For just this week, we want you to try to stop the wheels of activity for a limited period of time, and ask a vitally important question: what exactly is going on here?

Here's a good way to get started: At the end of each day—or, if you are an early-bird, the next morning right after you get up—reflect upon one event that stands out in your mind. It could be a conversation you had with a friend, a particularly interesting situation that occurred at work, an emotional reaction you had to someone or something, or some crazy image that popped into your mind. Take this one event and reflect on it as honestly as possible. Then write about it. Your writing could take the form of a journal entry, a piece of non-fiction, story-telling, or a bit of dialogue. It's that easy.

The key to writing effectively about what's going on in your life is to open your eyes to your life experiences or interactions with interesting people and then to record what you see, hear, or experience. Try to record these experiences and events in as much detail as possible, noting the specifics of what you observe. Your aim should be to give the reader— who could simply be you later on in life—as fully a realized portrait as possible of the event or events that you are describing. Spell out in detail what people were doing, saying, wearing, what their attitudes or feelings were (to the extent that you can ascertain them), and what the results of certain actions were. And, above all else, be sure to describe in depth your own feelings about what is going on in your life.

Writing About What's Going On in Your Life

To give you a sense of how this might work, let's use an example from

the life of college senior, Matt Reiber. Matt was asked to write about a
recent event that was significant to him, but all he could think of was an
experience he had running into a former girlfriend in a local bar. If Matt
was writing about the event in his journal, it might have looked something
like this:

Journal Entry
November 17, 2011

Went to Donnigan's last night for a beer with Adam. Dominga
was there with her friends, looking as hot as ever. Gave me a
look that really pissed me off, so I left the bar. Felt like shit the
whole night.

Given that nothing much happened in the event that Matt describes, one
would think that this would be a fairly poor experience to focus on for
creative writing. And yet, even with so little real drama to work with, Matt
was able to create a short piece that elevates the experience into something
much more interesting:

Cold Comfort
By Matt Reiber

She was looking at me from across the bar. It was a look of pity—
like I was some kind of pathetic loser or something. When I saw
that look on her face, it made me damn angry, not just because
of what she did to me, but because she thought that she still had
some kind of magical power over my heart.

She was without a doubt the hottest girl in the bar, and she
definitely knew it. Seeing her sitting there, looking so goddamn
fabulous, put me in a rotten state of mind because it reminded me
of just how much I missed her. It also made me realize that, after
what happened between us, I could never get her back. She had
already moved on and I was just a sad casualty of war.

"Go over and talk to her," my friend Adam urged me.

"No fucking way," I replied. "Let's just go somewhere
else."

As we got up to leave the bar, she glanced up at me again and
smiled. For a split second my resolve waivered and I was tempted
to reach out to her and try to put the past behind us. Then I came
to my senses.

"You'll never find another girl like that, Matt," Adam said in his usual idiotic way.

"Just wait and see," I said. "They'll be four or five more exactly like her in the next bar."

But even as a spoke these lines, I knew that they were a lie. There would never be anyone else like her. She knew it and I knew it.

I put on my jacket and walked outside the bar. It was only November, but the night was already bitterly cold. Cold, cold fucking night, and absolutely no chance it would get warmer any time soon.

By trying to give the reader a sense of what was going on in his mind while the events in the story were unfolding—his feeling of unrequited longing, his anger and frustration at his former girlfriend's callousness, and his desire for revenge—Matt transforms this event into something much more dramatic than it would seem at first glance. The inclusion of dialogue between himself and his friend, Adam, also helps to flesh out the experience for the reader.

Now it's time for you to do some reflecting on some of the recent experiences in your own life.

Exercise: What's Going On in Your Life?

Think over some of the events in your life during the past few weeks. Has anything interesting—or at least potentially interesting— happened that you can use as fodder for creative writing?

-

-

-

-

-

-

Past Tense: Reliving Memories

The life stories about which you choose to write don't have to be limited to what is going on in the present. You can also write about significant events that took place in the near or distant past. The reward of reflecting upon your past is that it can enable you to relive events that were delightful, powerful, or painful, while putting them into some kind of meaningful context. You might write about a first love, your first days of college, that amazing trip to Disney World when you were seven. Any event from the past that is still on your mind is proper fodder for these sorts of entries.

You can either write about these memories from your perspective at the time they occurred or from your place of greater wisdom in the present. That choice is up to you. Just be sure to write about these past experiences in as much vivid detail as possible.

Another major benefit of writing about your past while you still remember it is that, as you get older, these memories will inevitably begin to fade. When you are 50 you might remember the thrill of your first date with your teenage boyfriend, but you will probably have some difficulty remembering the specifics of that date or how you felt about it. That's why it's so important to take the time to try to get these memories down in as much detail as possible now while they are still somewhat fresh in your mind.

So many interesting things have probably happened to you during the course of your life, that you may have trouble deciding which of these to focus on in your writing. To help you narrow down your potential list of writing topics, we are going to employ a technique that is referred to as identifying the "Steppingstones" in your life.

Your Steppingstones

Dr. Ira Progoff in his *Intensive Journal* advises journal writers to make a list of the Steppingstones—or key events—in their lives. By Steppingstones Progoff is referring to:

those events that come to our minds when we spontaneously

reflect on the course that our life has taken from it's beginning to the present moment. The Steppingstones are the significant points of movement along the road of an individual's life. They stand forth as indicators of the inner connectedness of each person's existence, a continuity of development that maintains itself despite the vicissitudes and the apparent shifting of directions that occur in the course of a life....The special value...of Steppingstones... is that they...enable us to draw out of the jumbled mass of our life experiences the thin and elusive connective threads that carry our potentialities through their phases of development toward a fuller unfolding (76).

To put this in slightly more intelligible language, working with Steppingstones, according to Progoff, enables us to go back into our past in order to reconnect ourselves with those seminal experiences that helped make us who we are. The ultimate goal is not to linger on the past for its own sake, but to use this information to become more aware of the underlying continuity within our lives and, ideally, to allow this awareness to improve our future.

Now that you have some idea of what Steppingstones are all about, it's your turn to create your own list. In order to do this properly, Progoff recommends adopting a posture of relaxed awareness: close your eyes, sit silently, and allow your breath to flow softly and in a relaxed manner. Allow the events of your life to flow through your mind like a stream. If a particular event strikes your mind in a forceful manner, record it as a Steppingstone entry.

In constructing this list of Steppingstones, Progoff recommends that the journalist limit him or herself to no more than 12 entries, so that only the most significant events of one's life will rise to the surface. He encourages journalists to start with basic objective markers in their lives, such as birth, entering school, graduation, death of close relatives, marriage, and so on. These are recorded in chronological order as they happened. After that he advises moving on to more intimate and subjective Steppingstones. These more subjective Steppingstones might not seem so important to someone else, but they are events that had a major impact on you. For example, getting humiliated in the second grade, or not getting into the college of your choice.

At first, you can simply record as many Steppingstones as come to your mind in whatever order they appear. The key is to avoid censoring yourself when initially developing your list. Once you have a fairly detailed set of life markers, you can go back and arrange them in chronological order and then whittle them down to a list of the most significant 10 or 12. These are your Steppingstones.

To give you some idea of what your list of Steppingstones might look like, here is an example taken from Tristine Rainer's *The New Diary* (76):

1. I was born.
2. Around six my first real pain and scare in the hospital. I woke up during the tonsillectomy—inadequate anesthesia.
3. My first love—I was 15, Rose was 14.
4. College and an awareness of class distinctions, money, real competition.
5. Graduate school, the development of an aesthetic sophistication and effete elitism.
6. Marriage to Corinne—it seemed a perfect idea at the time.
7. Bought a movie camera and deemphasized graduate school. I began to make experimental films.
8. Divorce—Corinne left me in a way that I could not fail to get the message.
9. Marriage to Leah—this one really felt right!
10. Made a film in Greece and realization that my marriage was not right.
11. Boy born in London—so many complex emotions and conflicting desires.
12. Directed first feature-length film—low budget schlock, but I did it!
13. A beautiful daughter born—she had me from the moment I saw her....
14. Second marriage breaks up.

Now that you have some idea about how Steppingstones work, it's your turn to make a list of these important markers from your own life. Remember, you should try to limit yourself to 12 Steppingstones, so only the most significant events in your life should be included. Go ahead and give it a try.

Exercise
My Steppingstones

•

•

-

-

-

-

-

-

-

-

-

Working With Your Steppingstones

Once you decide which events from your past are worth exploring in writing, you should focus on one of these events and try, to the best of your ability to re-experience the event in as much detail and color as possible. Describing this practice, Progoff writes:

> We sit in stillness and close our eyes. Our breathing becomes slower and softer. We become quiet inside ourselves, letting our minds move back to the time of the Steppingstones Period. We do not deliberately try to recall any specific event, but we let ourselves *feel* into the atmosphere of that time in our lives. Gradually the atmosphere of that past time becomes present to us, and we feel the tone and quality and the circumstances of that period in our

experience. Now we can begin to record and describe the general aspects of what was taking place in our life at that time (94).

Having placed yourself as fully as possible in the atmosphere of the time in your life in which you are focusing, it is up to you to decide what form your writing about these events should take. You could describe your experiences in straightforward descriptive prose or write it as a story. Just let all the feeling, images, and reactions that come into your mind about this period flow onto paper. And above all, try not to be too self-conscious, self-critical, or self-censoring as you write.

Among the topics you may want to consider reflecting upon as you immerse yourself into your Steppingstone period are:

- What feelings did you have about yourself at this time?
- What kind of person were you at this time in your life?
- What kind of changes—if any—were you going through at this time?
- What was your attitude towards life at this time?
- Did you have any idea about what the future might hold in store for you?
- Did you have any special hopes or dreams about your future? (Progoff, 95)

Express Yourself

9.1. What's Going On Here. Take a few moments to recall one significant event from your previous day or week and write about it in a way that fully captures what you were experiencing at that time. Try to be as descriptive as possible in recounting the experience and be sure to include your reactions to the events that you are describing. To get started, try focusing on one or more of the following exercises:

9.1.1. Emotional Reaction. Has anything happened in your life recently that provoked a strong emotional reaction (jealousy, anger, fear, desire, sadness, passion)? Describe in detail the events that inspired this reaction and the outcome. If it's easier, you can write about the event in the second person as a flash fiction story.

9.1.2. The Extraordinary Ordinary. Choose a very mundane (boring) event that happened to you today and write in as much detail as possible about it. Your goal should be to make this event seem as fascinating as possible.

9.1.3. The Conversation. Record the details of an interesting conversation you had. You should try to capture the conversation in as much detail as possible so that your reader thinks that he is part of it.

9.1.4. Close Encounters. Every day we meet and interact with a wide variety of new people (cashiers, toll booth collectors, bank-tellers, customers). Select one interesting new person that you've interacted with recently. Describe the circumstances of your meeting and give your detailed impressions of that person. You can speculate as much and as wildly as you'd like about that person based upon your encounter with him or her.

9.2. Changes. Think of a significant change that you are going through right now in your life and explore it in as much detail as possible.

9.3. Catching Up. Write a letter to a friend with whom you've been separated and share some of the signficant things going on in your life right now. Be sure to send the letter to him or her!

9.4. Photo Memories. Go through some of your family photo albums and find a photo of yourself that speaks to you. Try using the photograph to help you remember details about the experience that was captured or ask an older member of your family to fill in some of the details. You could also just make up a story based upon the photography and allow your imagination to run wild.

9.5. I Remember. In 1975 artist and writer Joe Brainard catalogued memories of growing up in the 40s and 50s in the form of simple, declarative sentences, all beginning with, "I remember." Try writing your own version of "I Remember," listing 30-50 significant memories from your own childhood and adolescence. These memories don't have to be dramatic or even interesting. They just have to be significant to YOU and can include memories of events, food, clothing, people, toys, sorrows, joys, books, movies, music, places, images, etc.

9.6. Your Steppingstones. Choose one or more of the Steppingstones that you identified in this chapter. Following the practice that Progoff recommends for working with your Steppingstones, describe the experience in as much detail as possible. If you prefer, write a story about the experience.

9.7. The First Time. Tell the story about something significant you did for the first time (e.g., working a job, driving a car, the first day of high school or college).

9.8 Decisions. We are the products of the numerous choices that we make each and every day of our lives. Think back upon a time when you were forced to make an important decision that turned out badly. Describe that experience and what you learned from it (if anything).

9.9. Hard Times. Everyone goes through hard times in life, and you are no exception. Describe a time when you went through a hard time and what you were going through as you experienced it. If appropriate, you can also tell a story about this experience.

9.10. Going Wild. Describe or tell a story about a time when you went wild, when you did something completely wreckless or irresponsible. What prompted you to do this wild action? How did it all end? What were the consequences?

9.11. The Perfect Summer Vacation. Tell a story associated with a near-perfect summer vacation you once had. Where was it? Who were you with? What magical things happened to you?

9.12. Reimaginings. If you could take one event from your life and change it, what would it be? Now imagine what your new life would be like, positively and negatively, if you actually had the power to go back and change this event.

10

Supporting Characters

In the previous section of this text, we saw how the student, Pam, answered the question, "Who am I?" by first focusing on the various aspects of her persona. When pushed to elaborate a bit further, Pam then focuses on some of the intimate relationships in her life:

Who Am I?
(Part 2)
by Pam Pachedly

There are so many important people in my life that I hardly know where to begin. Of course my parents will always have a special place in my heart. I know I caused them a lot of heartache when I was growing up and I feel badly about that now. By the time I was about 14 I started hanging out with the wrong crowd, staying out late and experimenting with alcohol and pot. Sometimes I would come home really late after a night of partying and they would let me have it. There were more fights between my parents and me during those years then I care to remember. Through all of my idiotic behavior, though, my parents stood by me and supported me.

My sister, Sara, has always been my best friend, and I can confide in her about anything. She is two years older than I am, but we have always done everything together. When we were younger, we were the only girls on our block so we spent a lot of time playing together in the house. Later on, we went to different high schools, so we didn't spend as much time together as we used to. Now that we are at the same college, however, we see each other all the time and are even closer than we were as children.

I also have a few really good friends on the soccer team—Melanie, Chrissie, and Tanya in particular. Right now these three are the closest friends I have on earth. I went to elementary and high school with Melanie, so we go back a very long way. Although I've only known Chrissie and Tanya for a short while, we have so much in common that we all immediately became the best of friends. One thing I can say about all of my friends is that I can trust them no matter what. If that's not the definition of what a friend should be than I don't know what is!

Over the years I've dated more than my share of guys, but none of these relationships lasted all that long. I dated a guy named Glenn for over a year, but he turned out to be a complete asshole. He was so damned immature that he always preferred hanging out with his jackass friends to being with me. Eventually, I told him that he had to make a choice, and he did. Needless to say, he didn't choose me, which just goes to show you how big a loser he was. Sometimes I think that men in general are just immature jerks. For the time being, I'm very happy not to be in any kind of relationship.

As Pam realizes, any complete picture of a human being will necessarily include those individuals who have made a significant impact on his or her life. The intimate relationships we have with significant people in our lives help flesh out the portrait that we create of ourselves as persons and provide the raw material for really interesting creative products. Indeed without other people to interact with, to bounce ideas off of, to provide inspiration, creative activity would be extremely difficult, if not impossible.

People Who Need People

On a typical day, you probably interact with dozens of people. Most of the relationships we have with people are fairly casual relationships, or what used to be known as acquaintanceships. These sorts of relationships have a degree of superficiality about them that precludes us from emotionally investing ourselves in them. The young checkout girl in the supermarket who you see all the time, the people you interact with on a daily basis at work, or the accountant you meet once a year to help you with your taxes are usually not people whose happiness and well-being you give much thought about. You may not want to see these people miserable—any more than you would want to see any human being miserable—but you probably don't go out of your way to work for their ultimate welfare either. To use philosophical language, we normally use casual acquaintances as means to some higher goals that we have, and rarely are concerned with their own goals and needs per se.

There are, however, other people in our lives who we care about for their own sake. In these sorts of relationships of special significance, we typically regard the interests and goals of the other person as being at least as important as our own, and perhaps even more so. Their happiness becomes a source of our own happiness and their sadness becomes our sadness. In philosophical parlance, we view these people as "ends in themselves," never merely as means to some higher end.

The relationship of a mother to her child, for example, is one in which the mother's needs become totally subordinate to the needs of her child. The child's happiness and welfare is everything; the mother's a secondary consideration at best. The relationship of mother to child is probably the gold standard of all intimate relationships. But our relationships with close friends, for example, should ideally also be characterized by the same kind of selfless concern for them "for their own sakes" and not simply because of what we can get from them. Indeed, concern for the other for his or her own sake should probably be considered the hallmark of all intimate relationships as well as being the unique quality that separates relationships of special personal significance from the sort of casual relationships discussed earlier.

Love is All You Need

The word we commonly use to characterize the emotional content of these sorts of intimate relationships is "love." Unfortunately, the word "love" in our own times has come to take on a fairly vacuous connotation. We love our friends ("I really love you, man"); we love our Ipods; we even love potato chips. We claim to love so many things, our use of the word love itself has been rendered almost meaningless.

Erich Fromm, author of *The Art of Loving* sees part of the problem with our contemporary understanding of love stemming from a tendency to view love as a "pleasant sensation, which to experience is a matter of chance, something one 'falls into' if one is lucky" (1). If love is just something that "happens," then it doesn't require much work on our part. Fromm, therefore, prefers to view love as something that requires knowledge and effort to excel at—an art, just like any other art.

Fromm argues that human beings seek out love to help them overcome the feelings of separateness to which they are subject. The infant has a built-in sense of connectedness by virtue of contact with the mother. But once a person grows, this sense of connectedness becomes severed and she must look for a sense of connectedness in some other place—namely in the drive for interpersonal union with others. In love, writes Fromm, human beings achieve symbiotic union with others while still preserving their own individuality:

> Love is an active power in man; a power which breaks through the walls which separates man from his fellow men, which unites him with others; love makes him overcome his sense of isolation and separateness, yet it permits him to be himself, to retain his integrity. In love the paradox occurs that two beings become one and yet remain two. (17)

Of course, not all loving relationships succeed in this goal of allowing for connectedness while at the same time preserving individual identity. In some relationships, the individual's sense of isolation can actually increase or personal identity can actually be diminished. Indeed, the kind of idealized symbiotic union that Fromm describes is probably more of an ideal than a reality in the case of many of our intimate human relationships.

So Many Loves

Although in English we only have one word to characterize all the intimate relationships in our lives, the ancient Greeks had four terms which they believed described most of the loving relationships that human beings experience: *storge* (family affection), *philia* (friendship), *eros* (erotic love), and *agape* (love of God). For our purposes in this chapter, we are going to focus on the first three kinds of loving relationships and save *agape* for later in the program.

What *philia, storge, and eros* all have in common is that they move the bonds of love away from ourselves towards those who "belong to us"—those in our immediate sphere of concern. Self-love may be the first of all the loves we experience in life, but, unless we want to live in total emotional isolation, at one point or another, we must begin to extend our love to those nearest to us. These individuals become, as it were, almost an extension of our own personal identities. One always speaks of *my* child, *my* friend, *my* girlfriend in a way that indicates that those spoken about are viewed as part of oneself. This sense of the other as being somehow a part of ourselves may explain why we so readily come to the aid of family, friends, and sexual partners who need our assistance, but may not be quite as willing to assist others even though their objective needs might be greater.

All in the Family

The first place that most human beings experience love is within family life. As an infant, the first intimate bond a person has is with his mother, and it is through the relationship with his mother that the individual learns how to love. In *The Art of Loving*, Fromm maintains that a good parent always gives "the gift of milk and honey" to his or her child. "Milk" here refers to the parents' role in providing for the child's basic needs, life, and growth, while "honey" refers to their role in instilling in the child a love for living and a happiness at being alive. Fromm goes on to say that while most parents are capable of giving milk, not all are capable of giving honey, too (42).

Even children who grow up in fairly normal households often have conflicted feelings about their parents. We may love our parents but may also harbor unresolved resentment towards them. Perhaps they weren't always there when we needed them or maybe they didn't provide enough support when we were feeling vulnerable. As children become teenagers, they naturally desire to become more autonomous—to carve out their own domain in life apart from their parents. It's at this point that the teenager's desire for autonomy comes up against the parent's need to maintain some degree of control over their child's life—if only to protect them from a dangerous world. This tension between the teen's need for autonomy and the parent's desire for control is the cause of significant tension in most households.

Sigmund Freud, the founder of psychoanalysis, understood that childhood conflicts, mostly related to the relationship with one's parents, were at the root of most of the neuroses that his patients experienced. It's for this reason that during the course of therapy, Freud would often have patients try to relive traumatic experiences from their early life. Although dredging up painful experiences from childhood is never pleasant, it is certainly a useful exercise for beginning to work on unresolved emotional issues. These memories are also a goldmine for writers because the emotions associated with painful childhood experiences may be as intense in adulthood as they were during childhood.

Although *storge* technically refers to parental affection, we can broaden the concept to include the various kinds of love we have for all close family members. Depending upon how extended a family is this might also include siblings, grandparents, aunts and uncles, and possibly cousins. As with our relationship with our parents, dealings with other family members are often fraught with ambiguity. A sibling, for example, might be a best friend, but this doesn't mean that the relationship doesn't also contain its own fair share of jealously, envy, and spitefulness.

Critical examination of one's family life and upbringing is a vital step on the road to self-discovery. Who we are at present is shaped in great part by our past, and no part of our past is as formative as those crucial years of early family life. As you begin to reflect on your relationship to your family, powerful memories from your childhood will undoubtedly surface. Some of these memories will be delightful, others potentially painful. Our advice to you is to face these memories head on, to reflect deeply upon their significance, and above all, to write often about them. As was pointed out in an earlier chapter, these memories often get hazy with time. The time to write about them is when the memories and emotions associated with them are still fresh in your mind.

With Friends Like That

As Aristotle wrote in the fourth century BC, "No one would choose to live without friends, even if he had all other goods." For Aristotle, and indeed for most philosophers in the ancient world, friendship was considered one of the most important goods that we possess as human beings and necessary for human flourishing.

Although most of us intuitively recognize that our lives would be somewhat diminished without strong friendships, unlike other forms of love, friendship just doesn't seem quite as necessary. As C.S. Lewis once observed:

> Friendship is—in a sense not at all derogatory to it—the least *natural* of loves; the least instinctive, organic, biological, gregarious and necessary...Without [sexual love] none of us would have been begotten and without [parental love] none of us would have been reared; but we can live without Friendship. The species biologically considered, has no need for it (Lewis, 58).

Our contemporary lack of interest in the nature of friendship is unfortunate when you consider how much our friends influence us and how important they are to our ultimate well-being as human beings.

It was Aristotle who originally classified all friendships into three distinct categories: friendships of pleasure, friendships of utility, and friendships of virtue. In friendships of pleasure, two individuals are drawn to one another solely because of the enjoyment they derive from each other's company. The best example of this type of friendship would be drinking buddies or football pals, although some sexual relationships might also be included. Friendships of utility are founded in some practical benefit that friends perceive in their relationship with one another. In this sense, a business associate, a classmate who is part of a study group, or a neighbor with whom we carpool can legitimately be called friends, although our relationships with them might be limited to a specific domain of life (work, school, or the car).

In both friendships of pleasure and utility, people become friends because of what they can get out of the relationship and not necessarily because of any real affection that they have for one another. The focus in both cases is primarily on one's own needs, which can often make these kinds of friendships egocentric and in some cases exploitative. These kinds of friendships, according to Aristotle, are usually superficial at best and therefore fleeting.

There is another form of friendship that is a bit more substantial than the two kinds previously described. This third type, which Aristotle calls friendships of virtue, exists between two individuals who are drawn to one another for their own sake, and not simply what they can get out of the relationship (pleasure or some useful good). During the course of interacting with one another, something interesting happens to these kinds of friends: they actually improve each other's characters in profound ways. The reason why this sort of transformation occurs so naturally in friendships of virtue is because in such relationships, the friends are capable of acting as "mirrors" for each other's souls. By observing one's friend and seeing how he responds in difficult situations, one develops a more objective understanding of one's own nature, thus allowing for objective understanding of one's own character.

Although friendships of pleasure and utility might seem shallow compared to friendships of virtue, we probably need all three kinds of friendships to have rich and rewarding lives. It's also important to note that the number of friendships of virtue that we can have with other people will necessarily be limited because the intensity of this sort of relationship is quite demanding. On the other hand, we can have almost unlimited numbers of the more casual kinds of relationships that friendships of pleasure and utility provide. And we should never discount the psychological and spiritual lifts that such friendships can provide, despite their limited natures.

All three types of friendship also provide rich sources for the kinds of creative enterprises that we have been undertaking in this program. For many individuals—particularly those coming from troubled family lives—relationships with friends may be the most intimate that they have in their lives. Also, some of the most humorous, tragic, and poignant stories that we have probably involve each of the kinds of friends that Aristotle describes.

For Reflection

1. A happy memory associated with family members or friends was when...

2. A sad or painful memory associated with family members or friends was when...

3. An unresolved issue that I have with a particular family member or friend is....

4. A great adventure (or misadvanture) that I experienced with my family or friends was when...

Express Yourself

10.1. Portraits. Think of a family member or friend about whom you feel strongly. Picture the person in your mind, and try to conjure up as many details as possible about that person and your feelings towards him or her. Write character sketch of this person that is so vivid that a reader can picture the person clearly in his or her mind after reading your piece. Be sure to include as much descriptive detail about this person as you can to flesh out your character sketch. Or, if you prefer, write a poem about this person that expresses your true feelings towards him or her.

10.2. All in the Family. In the previous chapter of this text, you were asked to tell some of the important stories of your life. Some of these stories undoubtedly centered around your family life. If you have any more interesting stories about people in your family, tell them now. As you write, keep in mind that as people get older, they begin to forget their great family stories. Think of this as your opportunity to capture a piece of family history before it gets lost in the fog of age.

10.3. Family Tradition. Describe a tradition that is unique to your family. Be sure to explain your own feelings about this tradition (i.e., do you value it or is it just a burden to you). If you prefer, you can tell a story related to this tradition.

10.4. Holiday Gatherings. Holidays can be times of immense joy or times of incredible stress, depending upon how you relate to your family. Write about a holiday gathering that was particularly significant to you.

10.5. Friendly Tales. During the course of your life, you've probably had many deep, significant friendships with interesting people. Try telling some of the interesting stories about your friends. Here are just a few possibilities:

10.5.1. Tell a story about how you met a close friend.

10.5.2. Tell a story about the incidents surrounding the end of a longstanding friendship.

10.5.3. Tell a story about a time when you felt betrayed by a close friend.

Of course, if you prefer, any of the above exercises can be written as poems or as letters to the friends involved in the incidents you've described.

10.6. Getting Reacquainted. Has there been a close friend in your life with whom you've lost contact? If so, write a letter to that person telling what he or she meant to you. You can also feel free to remind that person about some special time that the two of you shared together.

10.7. Role Models. Is there a family member or friend who has served as a mentor or role model for you? Describe your relationship with this person and how it benefitted you. Or, if there is an interesting story related to this person, tell it.

10.8. Dealing with Sickness. Have you ever had a loved one who was going through a prolonged period of serious illness? If so, write about this sickness and how it affected you as you went through it with the person involved.

10.9. Saying Goodbye. Quite often in life friends and family members die before we can tell them how we feel about them. If you've had this experience, write a letter to this person expressing your feelings about them. Try to imagine that they are still able to read your letter, and write it accordingly.

10.10. Furry Friends. If you've had an intimate friendship with a member of another species, tell a story or write a poem about this creature or your relationship with it.

11

The Pangs of Eros

We have seen that many of the most interesting stories in a person's life related to interactions with intimate others. Our relationships with family members and friends, because they are often so emotionally charged, provide constant fodder for creative expression. But, if you were to examine most of the novels, plays, or poems that have been written throughout the centuries, the one sort of relationship that out-strips all others in terms of its potential to inspire both the heart and mind is known in Greek as *eros*—erotic love.

When we hear the world "erotic," most of us almost automatically think of sex. But in his work, *The Four Loves*, C.S. Lewis makes the distinction between *eros*—which he refers to as "being in love"—and sexual activity. He points out that one could engage in sexual activity apart from *eros* (with a prostitute, for example, or on a one night stand) and *eros* can certainly exist apart from sexual intimacy (in Platonic or unrequited love, for example) (91). In general, however, when we talk about *eros*, there will usually be some kind of physical manifestation of the attraction that a couple feels for one another: kisses, caresses, and, yes, sex are usually part and parcel of what it means to be "in love". In fact, for most couples, the desire for sexual contact with the other precedes the act of falling in love, as Lewis also observes. We desire to fondle first and love only later.

Erich Fromm describes erotic love as "the craving for complete fusion, for union with one other person." It's this craving for union, he argues, that separates *eros* from all other forms of love. *Eros*, unlike family love or friendship, is by its very nature exclusive. We can certainly love multiple children or multiple friends. But true *eros*, writes Fromm, demands exclusivity (44).

The experience of "falling in love," "being in love" and "wanting to be in love" are probably among the most complex emotional states that many of us will ever experience in life. Perhaps you can recall the first time you really fell for someone. Every time you saw that person—at the beginning of the relationship, at least—your heart probably skipped a beat, your palms might have become sweaty, and you may have even been at a loss for what to say to him or her. There's nothing in the world like the experience of forming an intense emotional and physical attraction to another human being. It's probably for this reason, even in old age, after they forget just about everything else, many people can vividly recall their first romantic relationship.

The thing about erotic relationships, however, is that they can take on a bewildering variety of forms. From the spiritual love of Dante and Beatrice in the *Divine Comedy* to the whips and chains of the Marquis de Sade, erotic love is essentially a diverse phenomenon that comes in many different flavors. Here are just a few of the varieties of *eros* as evidenced in the reflections of typical college students:

Unrequited Eros

> *When I first met Gary there was something about him that drove me completely insane. I don't know exactly what it was. The first time I saw him, he was sitting in a desk waiting for our English class to start. He was doodling mindlessly in his notebook. Every once in a while he would turn around to see what the rest of us in the class were doing. His eyes were an amazing shade of blue, and when his eyes met mine, I felt like there was an explosion in my chest. I spent most of that semester day-dreaming about him and about being with him. At the same time, though, I also knew that he was way out of my league. The pain of that feeling made me want to cry every time I went to English class.   (Jillian, 19)*

Of all the types of *eros*, unrequited love has undoubtedly been the most celebrated in poetry and song throughout much of human history. From the ancient Greek lyric poets to the sappy pop tunes of our present age, this sort of love is often treated as one of the formative experiences of human beings.

When love is described as "unrequited," what we mean is that it is unreturned and often unrecognized. We pine for the object of our desire, while at the same time realizing that this object will probably remain out of our reach. This is not to say that we don't desire to have our love recognized and reciprocated, but there's something about the object of our desire that makes it unattainable. To use baseball metaphors, the object might be described as "out of our league" (too good for us), "off for the season" (unavailable for whatever reason), or "plays for a different team" (is attracted to the "wrong" gender). If these conditions could somehow be changed, reciprocal love might be possible and a real relationship could be pursued. But the existence of one or more of these conditions means that desire will inevitably only be able to flow in one direction. In some cases, the object of our love may not even know we desire him or her. Gary, for example, probably has absolutely no idea that Jillian has a thought about him, and would probably be surprised to hear about how she feels.

The fact that this form of love is not reciprocated lends unrequited love a tragic quality. The person whose feelings go unreturned suffers—often intensely, dramatically, and exquisitely. If you've ever been around someone going through this kind of experience, you probably know that their reactions can often be like something out of an overblown Italian opera. It has been said that those who are involved in unrequited love experience as much pain as someone going through the breakup of a romantic relationship without ever having the benefit of being in that relationship. More often than not, one is willing to accept his or her suffering as the price of experiencing the intense feelings of passion that come with longing for the other.

The advantage of this type of love, of course, is that by keeping one's feelings to oneself, one never has to experience rejection. Nor does one have to experience the diminishment of the admirable qualities of the object of desire that often occurs in normal relationships, because that object retains its idealized form precisely by not being in a flesh-and-blood relationship.

Physicalized Eros

I'd been wanting and waiting to get Jackie alone in my room for days, but my roommate, Steve, was always hanging around with his lame-ass friends from the college bowl. Finally, one night I had managed to get him out of our room for a few hours and invited Jackie over. She was wearing a very tight dress that showed off her incredibly hot body. I could sense that she was waiting for this moment as much as I was, and it didn't take long for me to maneuver her into my lower bunk bed.

The room was completely dark and we were under my covers kissing and rubbing our bodies together. I knew that this was my moment and if I didn't make my move now, I'd never have a chance like this again. I ran my fingers under her dress and behind her back, looking for the clasp to her bra. Fumbling. More fumbling. She was giggling, but offering me no real help. Finally, the clasp came undone, and I moved quickly to go for the prize.

At that very moment I heard a key in the door to my room. The lights came on suddenly and in walked my asshole roommate Steve with five of his college bowl buddies. Jackie giggled self-consciously and put her bra back on. She was out of the room in a heartbeat, too self-conscious even to say goodbye.

"Did we come at the wrong time?" Steve asked, completely oblivious to the mortal damage that he had just caused me.

All I could do was pull the sheets over my head and bite my knuckles to avoid screaming.

"Anyone up for a game of Risk?" Steve asked.   (Kevin, 20)

For the true romantic involved in unrequited love, the physical attainment of the object of desire is almost besides the point. To be able to act upon one's feelings of desire is viewed by the romantic as a kind of crass betrayal of his or her love. But there is also a type of lover who relishes almost exclusively in the pleasure that contact between two bodies can produce—one who delights in the actual attainment of sexual gratification.

Although the ancient Greeks delighted in writing poems celebrating sexual love, for much of our Western history depictions of this sort of love were considered taboo. It was only in the mid-twentieth century with the flowering of the sexual revolution and the women's movement that artists began to relish in realistic depictions of human sexuality. Today the erotic—in the more narrow sense of sexual love—is considered respectable enough to be represented by its own section in middle American bookstores.

The vestiges of Manichaeanism, however, occasionally still surface in our society. The Manichaeans were a heretical group in the Middle Ages that believed that the body and sexuality were evil and that if one wanted to be saved it was important to live a completely spiritual—that is sex-free life. Although Manichaeanism was condemned by the Church, it managed to influence our Western ways of thinking about the body and sexuality perhaps more than we care to realize. In the West, for the most part, the body is something that is supposed to be covered up and sex is something that is best not talked about in "polite company."

In the Christian tradition sex is traditionally viewed primarily as a means to some higher end—procreation, for example, or as an expression of the love that a couple feels for one another. The problem with this sort of means-end approach to sex is that sex itself is only considered morally acceptable if it is connected with some loftier purpose.

But sex can also be understood, as philosopher Alan Goldman simply as "the desire for contact with another person's body and for the pleasure that such contact produces" (251). This approach makes sex an end in itself with no higher goal than the pleasure that it produces in the couple that partakes in it.

In the selection above, Kevin has one goal and one goal alone. When he is interrupted from his quest for physical intimacy with Jackie, he is clearly pissed off. Jackie may be slightly embarrassed at being caught *in flagrante delicto*, but he definitely is not. And it can almost be guaranteed that the moment that he has the opportunity to act on his desires again, he will most certainly do so.

Dysfunctional Eros

Did I actually love Tiffany? That's a really tough question. I loved her and I hated her at the same time. When we were alone together, there was no one I loved more in the world. She was so amazingly beautiful, it would almost drive me to the point of insanity.

But Tiffany often used her body as a weapon to make me suffer. When she wanted to, she could be the most sadistic bitch in the entire universe. She would get me to the point where I was so aroused that I felt like I was going to explode and then she would suddenly stop and say she didn't feeling like going any further. She did that a lot.

When we were out, she'd also make it a point to flaunt her stuff around other guys, just to get a reaction out of me. I'd watch her dancing with some dumb jock—dancing really close. Then she would turn to look at me with a sadistic smirk on her face. When I would complain about it afterwards, she'd laugh and tell me I was a jealous idiot.

Things went on like that for about eight months. I wanted to break up with her, but she'd pulled all the strings in our relationship. The only reason why I'm not with her right now is that she found some other loser to dick around.

Man, I really miss her so much. (Tony, 18)

Not every relationship is a pure as unrequited love or as direct as sexual conquest. Many intimate relationships are also wrapped up in some degree or another of dysfunction. A dysfunctional relationship is one in which the relationship itself or the desire that motivates it causes misery for both of the parties involved.

Naturally, these more volatile, conflict-ridden sorts of erotic relationships are extremely interesting as objects of creative exploration (even if they are sources of endless anguish to those who actually experience them). No film, novel, or play, for example, could ever be sustained if their plots revolved around two individuals who are totally in love with one another in a pure and selfless way. That would be mind numbingly boring for most of us. That's why all the greatest stories about erotic relationships always center around turmoil, intrigue, and disintegration. Without some sort of conflict or difficulties, romantic tales become trite and uninteresting.

It's certainly the case that one can have sex apart from love, one can have sexual relations with multiple partners, one's sexual activity could simply be a way of using another person as an object, and one's sexual desire could border on the perverse. There are also highly dysfunctional sorts of sexual relationships in which partners manipulate, abuse, or try to control one another. Sexual activity can express itself in a relationship in a myriad of ways, not all of which are healthy or emotionally satisfying... but, we would have to acknowledge that they are all fairly interesting, to say the least.

Is there any doubt at all that Tony would still be with Tiffany if she didn't discard him first? And what exactly was the basis of their relationship when they were together? It certainly appears to be the classic sadist-masochist type of relationship in which the masochist (Tony) desires pleasure from the suffering and pain caused by the sadist (Tiffany), who in turn desires her own pleasure from the dispensing of such suffering and pain. All we need to do is add some whips and chains and Tony and Tiffany's relationship would become something right out of the Marquis de Sade!

Of course, all erotic relationships are dysfunctional in their own way. The difference is often merely a matter of degree.

Ruptured Eros

You want to know about endings? I can tell you everything that you've ever wanted to know. I'm a master at endings. It's beginnings and middles that I have trouble with.

Paul and I started dating while we were in high school. We had been friends for a few years when he first proposed that we go out together. I was a bit surprised by this, because I never thought of him in that way. But I always got along well with him, and I figured, what the hell, at least we'll have some fun together.

One thing led to another, and by the end of junior year we were definitely an item. Most of our friends thought we made the perfect couple. There was only one problem: it was called college.

Paul was thinking about going for Pre-Med and there were no schools in our area with a decent program. I really need to stay close at home, because my mother was going through chemo therapy for breast cancer and I wanted to be by her side during her treatments.

Things were fine for the first year. I went up to Boston at least one weekend a month to stay with him and he came home to be with me all the time. By the middle of sophomore year, though, things had started to change. Paul didn't seem to have as much time for me as he used to. He said it was because of all the work he had to do for his Pre-Med program, but my gut told me that something else was going on.

Eventually, the truth came out. He had fallen for some bimbo that he met in one of his classes and had been cheating on me for at least six months. He said that it had nothing to do with me (Why do all guys insist on using that idiotic line?), but I was completely torn apart by our break-up. For the rest of the semester, I couldn't think about anything but him—not my school work, not my friends, not even my poor mother. I was like a walking zombie. I still haven't gotten over Paul completely, and when the phone rings, I keep thinking that it will be him, calling to say that he wants to come back to me. What a sad, pathetic loser I am! (Grace, 21)

No one wants an intimate relationship to fall apart, but the sad truth is that most relationships end before one or both of the parties involved want them to. If that wasn't the case, everyone would be married to their teen sweethearts and no one would ever get divorced. And yet, we know that most young people will probably have numerous break-ups in their lives and the majority of marriages now end in divorce. It would seem that the odds are that if you are in any kind of relationship with a significant other that your relationship has a fairly good chance of ending unhappily.

The agony of a broken relationship—whether it is caused by one party moving on, by mutual consent, or by the death of a loved one—is probably one of the most intense experiences any of us will ever have. Although there certainly are some couples that break up amicably and are able to remain friends, the intense emotions involved in erotic relationships all but ensure that that their endings will be as acrimonious as their beginnings were rapturous.

And the emotional pain of these relationships can linger far longer than it reasonably should. Grace, for example, was a senior when she wrote about her experiences with Paul. Their relationship ended a year-and-a-half earlier, and she still bears the scars from that experience. But like the other sorts of intense erotic relations that we have examined, unintended endings also provide interesting fodder for creative expression. Second only to unrequited *eros*, ruptured *eros* claims a place of prominence as the predominant theme of most of the love songs written in the past sixty years.

As you can see from all these examples, there is no such thing as a monolithic or universal type of *eros*. Each individual will express his or her sexual identity in a way that is purely unique; each couple will act out their sexual desires in a similarly unique fashion. From the insatiable longings of the teenage couple who engage in hours of surreptitious groping and kissing while adults are out of the house to the elderly couple who barely have enough energy or passion left in their relationship to hold hands any longer, the one thing we can say about *eros* is that it captures the full diversity of the human experience. And, if nothing else, sexual desire and intimacy will always be a fascinating object of exploration.

For Reflection

Think about the most significant romantic or sexual feelings that you've had during the course of your life. It's not necessary that you acted upon these feelings, only that they were important to you at the time. Reflect on the following questions as you go through your self-exploration:

1. What were the circumstances in which these feelings arose?

2. What was it about this person that aroused these feelings (be specific)?

3. What sort of emotions did you experience at the time (again, be specific)?

4. How did you choose to act (or not act) upon these emotions? What was the outcome?

Express Yourself

11.1. My First Crush. Write about the first crush you had for someone and how it went.

11.2. The Magical First Date. If you've had one of these, write about it in detail. Descibe how the date came about, what was involved, what the weather was like, what you were wearing, all the incredible things that happened from beginning to end.

11.3. True Love. Think back upon the great love of your life (if you've had one) and write a romantic poem idealizing this relationship.

One of the most enduring poetic styles for this type writing is the ballad. Ballads are nothing more than stories told in verse form and are often used to write contemporary pop songs. Although ballads can take many different forms, the most popular is the four line stanza in which the second and forth lines rhyme. Here's an example taken from *Poetry for Dummies*:

> The winter moon has tipped and spilled
> Its shadows on the lawn
> When Farmer Owen woke to find
> His only daughter gone;
>
> She'd taken all the clothes she had
> Against the biting cold,
> And in a note to him she wrote,
> "I've taken all your gold."

Although you can use ballads to tell almost any story, they are particularly appropriate for stories of love and the dissolution of love. The form of a ballad is a bit more structured than other poetic forms that we have examined, but it's easy enough for novice poets and would-be songsmiths.

Of course, if you don't like the restrictive struture of the ballad, then feel free to write your poem the way you want. Remember, there are no hard and fast rules here, only gentle suggestions.

11.4. Premature Endings. Tell a story about a romantic encounter (or potential romantic encounter) that ended prematurely or that left you feeling frustrated.

11.5. The Bitter Agony. Almost everyone at one point or another in their lives has had the experience of feeling used, abused, neglected, or cheated upon by a romantic partner. The bitter memories of this kind of experience often linger with people for many years afterwards. If you've had this kind of experience in your life, write about it in the form of a story, a poem, or a dialogue between you and your partner. Feel free to express any emotions that may surface as you reflect upon this experience.

11.6. Love Letter. Write a romantic or steamy love letter to your significant other (if you have one) or your unrequited love telling them everything you feel about them. If you prefer, you can write a letter to a famous person who you are attracted to just for fun.

11.7. Wild Fantasies. Try your hand at some stream-of-consiousness writing about a romantic or erotic fantasy of yours. Take this anywhere you'd like...just follow your passions whereever they lead you and try not to be too self-conscious about what you are writing.

11.8. Forbidden Love. Have you ever been attacted to someone who you knew was either no good for you (for whatever reason) or who you knew would be disapproved of by your friends or family? If so, write about this experience and how it affected you.

Uncovering
the Real Me

Congratulations! You've made it through the first three parts of The Creative Self Program, and have now come to the fourth and most important part—the meat and potatoes of the program, if you will. This is the time when you will be asked to dig deep inside yourself and confront aspects of your personal identity that you may not even know exist…or perhaps don't want to know exist.

For the sake of continuity, let's look back at what we've been doing during the past few weeks and see how it will tie in with what we will be doing from this point forward.

During the first part of the program (Weeks 1-4), you were shown a technique known as concentrated awareness that we asked you to use to begin looking at the world around you in a more introspective way. You began by focusing on the mundane, seemingly boring, objects around you—an old wrench, withered flowers in your front yard, your messy closet—to try to find the inner beauty and magesty in these things.

During the second part of the program (Weeks 5-8), you were then asked to apply the technique of concentrated awareness to your persona or the mask you wear to interact with the outer world. During this part of the course, you explored in as much detail as possible your physical appearance, personality, and your attiudes and beliefs. Perhaps you even discovered things about these aspects of yourself that you never even realized before.

From the *persona*, you moved, in the third part of the program (Weeks 9-11), to the great stories of your life, both those that are unfolding in the present and those that have unfolded in the past. You also explored those relationships with intimate others—family, friends, and lovers—that add richness and texture to your life stories.

By now you should have several pieces of writing, including some straightforward prose, some poems, some flash-fiction, and perhaps even a dialogue or two. You may even have some interesting photos that you've taken or perhaps some art that you've created to go along with these pieces. If you've done that much, you are completely on target. There's no right or wrong in this program. Provided you've captured a bit of who you are as a person in your writing and photography, then you are doing just fine.

The first three parts of this program focused almost exclusively on your outer life—the "you" that is readily visible to others. Now we are going to shine the spotlight on your inner self. This is where things get a bit tricky. You see, most of us spend the bulk of our conscious life focused outward. We usually prefer to ignore the stuff that lies inside of us because introspection is either too difficult or too painful.

Let's be honest here: what we have been doing up until now in this program is simply skimming the surface of your personal identity. The REAL you is much more than those superficial aspects of your personality that you so readily project onto the external world. The real you is the painful, dark baggage you carry around inside yourself—your deep hurts, fear and anxieties, your dark, festering, often unrealized longings, your violent rages and hates. It's all the stuff you definitely prefer that others not know about you, because you are terribly afraid that, if others see the heavy baggage you carry inside you, they will reject you outright. And, indeed, perhaps they might.

Of course, there is another side of the real inner you, too. This is the you that is wild and whimsical, totally free and totally spontaneous. It's the you that carries a bright and shining spark of the divinity deep inside itself and which is harmoniously connected with the primal stuff of the universe. This luminescent and transcendent side of each human being also exists but it rarely has the opportunity to shine forth because, sadly, it is usually totally neglected by us.

So now it's time to remove the blinders that prevent us from fully examining our inner selves. The writing that you will be asked to do now is certainly more difficult than in earlier chapters. I promise, however, that if you take the time to dig deep inside yourself and fearlessly face whatever you encounter—no matter how painful or frightening it might be—you will discover an amazing font of creative inspiration.

And who knows: you might just learn one or two new things about yourself in the process!

12

The Wounded Child

ost human beings would rather do just about anything else in life than focus on painful memories and childhood traumas. And yet that is exactly what we are going to ask you to do in this part of the program. You might think that it is a bit sadistic of us to intentionally make you dwell on your deep inner wounds, anxieties, and fears, but there is a purpose to this that will become evident as you work your way through this chapter. All we ask you to do is to have faith and see what happens.

Earlier in this text, you were encouraged to tell some of the wonderful stories of your life. If you are like most people, the stories you probably focused on were the pleasant ones. And, hopefully, you had more than enough happy stories from your life to share.

But if you were to be honest with yourself, you would have to acknowledge that—unless you grew up in some kind of fantasy land—your life story is probably also filled with more than its fair share of unpleasant, difficult, dissatisfying moments. The very act of being born is a traumatic experience for an infant (How many babies do you know who are born laughing?). From that moment on, we have to live with all sorts of stresses, miseries, regrets, and losses. By the time most people get to their teenage years, they are bundles of anxieties, neuroses and insecurities. We may try to suppress some of these painful aspects of our identities, but they are always still there, emerging when we least expect it.

Think about it logically. If most people are so damned happy, then why are self-help books an ever-growing multimillion-dollar industry? Why are so many people in therapy looking for answers to their problems? Why are antidepressants one of the largest growing segments of the pharmaceutical industry? Finally, if life is so incredibly wonderful, then why do so many people try to escape from it by abusing drugs and alcohol?

No matter how diligent your parents may have been when you were growing up, there's no possible way that they could have satisfied all of your physical and emotional needs. Most have more than their own share of emotional baggage to deal with and do the best they can raising children. The result, in many cases, is years of often-unintentional emotional neglect, lack of sufficient affection, and the failure of parents to provide adequate boundaries for their children.

The Wounded Inner Child

This vulnerable, hurt, frightened part of each of us that was never able to fully express its deepest feelings, longings, and anxieties is what some psychologists have come to refer to as the wounded inner child. John Bradshaw, one of the authorities on this subject, describes the characteristics of an adult with a wounded inner child as one who...

- is out of touch with his feelings, needs, and desires.
- engages in reckless and irresponsible behavior.
- has narcissistic and insatiable craving for love, attention and affection.
- has a deep-rooted sense of distrust and a corresponding inability to attain intimacy with other people.
- acts out in rage or inappropriate behavior or "acts in" with excessive self-criticism.
- has a propensity to engage in addictive and compulsive behavior, which can include alcohol or drug abuse, but also addictions to work, shopping, sex, or gambling (Bradshaw, 21).

The wounded inner child might come into being for a number of different reasons. Some individuals were not allowed to express their true feelings as children; others were forced to conform to the expectations of others ("You have to be serious about life!"); still others may have been forced to grow up too quickly or to take on too much responsibility at a young age. The typical cause is emotional neglect or abuse during childhood. But, as Bradshaw points out, it can also result from being overly pampered as a child, which gives certain individuals the beliefs that they deserve special treatment from everyone and can do no wrong (Bradshaw, 11).

You might be thinking right now that this discussion about the wounded inner child does not apply to you in any way. And you may be right. Perhaps you had the perfect childhood with parents who were keenly attuned to your physical and emotional needs. Perhaps you really are extremely happy and well satisfied with life and don't suffer from any sort of anxieties, fears, longings, regrets, or recriminations. If that's the case consider yourself very fortunate indeed.

Most people, however, have a wounded child within them to one degree or another. An extreme case would be the person who is so battered by life, so neglected or abused, that he engages in a persistent pattern of self-destructive behavior throughout his life. At the other end of the spectrum is the person who, as we have seen, really is completely and totally at peace with his or her life. Most human beings probably lie somewhere in between on the spectrum. They've been wounded just enough during childhood that some degree of insecurity, fear, or pain colors their adult lives. For such individuals, the only cure for the scars they carry inside them, is to get in touch with their own wounded inner child, as unpleasant as the prospect of that encounter might sound.

Getting In Touch with Your Wounded Inner Child

You are probably wondering why on earth you would want to do this. After all, wouldn't it be much better to let sleeping dogs lie and try to forget, as much as possible, whatever pains and traumas we experienced during childhood? The problem with this approach is that, although you may prefer to ignore your wounded inner child, he demands attention. You can try to ignore him, but you do so at your own peril.

On a more positive note, owning our inner wounds allows us the possibility for release of the negative energy and destructive emotions that are driving us. That's the reason why so many people choose to participate in therapy. Sessions with a counselor or psychologist may not be fun, and some of the wounds that these sessions dredge up may be downright painful. But, by dealing with their emotional baggage openly and honestly, many therapy patients find an emotional release that would not have otherwise been available to them.

Although therapy is definitely appropriate for individuals carrying around severe traumas from childhood, there is another method of getting in touch with the wounded inner child that is readily available to all of us. It's called writing. If you've been keeping a journal through the years and are honest about your experiences, you've probably been dialoging with your inner child without even realizing it.

There's no doubt that writing about painful experiences is difficult.

The emotions that can arise while you are writing about these kinds of experiences can seem overwhelming. As a starting point, Tristine Rainer recommends the following approach to facilitate the writing process:

> Articulate as much as you can, even your barely formulated thoughts and fears. Allow yourself to cry as you write, if you feel the need. Write until you can write no more; write until you are exhausted. The more deeply you can express your pain, the sooner you will work through it.
>
> Don't make judgments about yourself or your writing when you are feeling intensely. Don't be afraid that you will uncover more pain than you are able to cope with. You will go only as deeply as you can at any one time, because people working on their own...have natural resistances and defenses beyond which they will not push themselves. You also need not fear that confronting and expressing the pain will create more pain. If you have pain inside, the articulation and the accompanying emotion help you to move through it. The only suffering that does not move from pain to ease is suffering that is blocked in some way. (117)

As Rainer observes, pent up emotions fester and ultimately become obsessions. In this respect, writing can serve a cathartic function. Expressing painful emotions allows you to acknowledge them, and ultimately allows you to put some distance between yourself and the emotion. This is when relief from what is troubling you starts to happen.

Below are a few techniques that you could use to make the process of dealing with your painful memories and feelings much more focused and intentional. If you feel comfortable, try them; if not, feel free to move on to some other topics for writing.

Regression Exercise

Through the process of regression, we take ourselves back in time to the period when most of our emotional scars were formed—early childhood—and intentionally try to re-experience the situation that caused these scars.

1. *Begin by sitting comfortably in a dark, quiet room. Take a few deep breaths and allow your mind to relax.*
2. *Now imagine yourself as a child between the ages of three and eight. Picture yourself with your family. What emotions*

*are you experiencing? Are you happy or sad? Content or
disappointed? Peaceful or insecure?*
3. *Now write about what you've experienced. Stream-of-
consciousness writing is ideal for this sort of exercise
because it prevents self-sensoring.*

Regression can be an extremely potent technique, and you should be very
careful about what sorts of painful memories it can dredge up. If done
regularly, regression could even surface traumatic memories that you
repressed as a child because they were too difficult for you to handle at
the time.

Primal Therapy

In the early 1970s a psychologist named Arthur Janov developed a
therapeutic technique that came to be known as primal therapy. Janov
believed that the cause of neuroses or emotional pain has its origins in
some sort of childhood trauma. The child, unable to handle the trauma,
represses it. Janov thought that the repressed pain could be brought to
consciousness by reliving the incident that caused it and fully expressing
the resulting pain. By confronting the trauma in a therapeutic setting,
Janov believed that the trauma could ultimately be resolved.

One of the most famous individuals to attempt this sort of therapy
was John Lennon. In the 1970s, the group that Lennon had founded, the
Beatles, had recently broken up, and Lennon was in the grips of a painful
heroin addiction and crippled by personal and professional insecurities.
He turned to primal therapy in a belief that the source of many of his
problems stemmed from the painful experiences he had as a child, most
notably his separation from his mother, Julia, and her tragic accidental
death during his teenage years. During an interview, Lennon candidly
discussed his primal therapy sessions:

> There's no way of describing it, it all sounds so straight just
> talking about it, what actually you do is cry. Instead of penting
> up emotion, or pain, feel it rather than putting it away for some
> rainy day..... I think everybody's blocked, I haven't met anybody
> that isn't a complete blockage of pain from childhood, from birth
> on...... It's like somewhere along the line we were switched off not
> to feel things, like for instance, crying, men crying and women
> being very girlish or whatever it is, somewhere you have to switch
> into a role and this therapy gives you back the switch, locate it and
> switch back into feeling just as a human being, not as a male or a

female or as a famous person or not famous person, they switch you back to being a baby and therefore you feel as a child does, but it's something we forget because there's so much pressure and pain and whatever it is that is life, everyday life, that we gradually switch off over the years. All the generation gap crap is that the older people are more dead, as the years go by the pain doesn't go away, the pain of living, you have to kill yourself to survive. This allows you to live and survive without killing yourself.

Like regression, primal therapy is a powerful experience that is best attempted in a professional setting. Once you start to elicit traumatic memories, you really never know where this process will ultimately lead. For some writers, however, the process of tapping into traumatic memories from the past can be quite liberating. If you feel comfortable enough, try the following limited form of primal reflection:

Primal Therapy Exercise

1. *Begin by sitting comfortably in a dark, quiet room. Take a few deep breaths and allow your mind to relax.*
2. *Think back to a painful memory from your childhood. Try to allow your mind to fully relive the experience that caused you pain. Now feel the emotions that were present at the time. Allow yourself to express these emotions any way you want (e.g., through tears, screams, pounding the floor, etc.).*
3. *Now write about what you've just experienced.*

Although primal therapy has fallen out of favor since the 1970s, there's no doubt that Janov was onto something when he encouraged patients such as Lennon to fully experience the childhood pain that they had repressed, rather than simply ignoring it. But unlocking these emotions that may have been repressed for so long can also be profoundly disturbing for some people. If you find that this is the case for yourself, consider finding a professional to talk through some of the issues that may have surfaced from this exercise.

For Reflection

The words that best describe my childhood are...

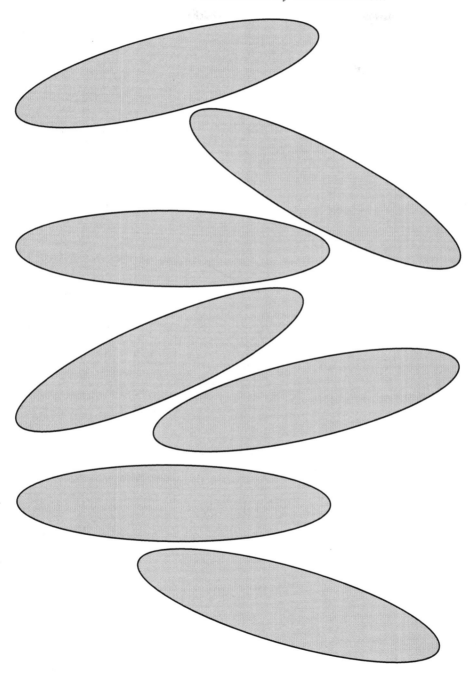

Express Yourself

The following exercises require you to go deep inside yourself, exploring painful emotions that are often left unexpressed. In some cases, you will be asked to "make your writing cry"—or, to put this in more understandable terms, to reconnect with the wounded child within you who is fearful, upset, insecure or full of pain and hurt. There is a real value in exploring those places that hurt inside ourselves, but it certainly takes great courage and strength to make the effort.

Any of the following exercises can be done in prose, poetry or as dialogues. If it's easier for you, you can use second person voice when writing ("he said;" "she said") or write any of these as a story, allegory, or fairy tale. The choice is completely up to you.

One caveat before you begin these exercises: Although it's important to try to move beyond your comfort zone when writing about emotionally laden topics, it's also important not too push yourself too far before you are ready. If you find that any of these exercises are too difficult for you, feel free to skip them and work on earlier exercises in this text. If you're like most people, however, you may find it somewhat therapeutic to attempt this sort of writing.

12.1. Heart Scars. This exercise is adapted from G. Lynn Nelson's *Writing and Being* (112). In an earlier exercise, you were asked to describe your physical scars; now you will examine your emotional scars, which are not quite as obvious to others. Take a deep breath and quiet yourself. Think about all the deep hurts, the traumas of the heart, that you experienced during the course of your life. Some of these will be obvious (the death of a loved one, your parents' divorce); others will be more subtle (not making it into honors in high school). Feel free to list all these heart scars and choose one that you feel was particularly painful and explore it, examine it in detail, feel it again.

12.2. Life Stresses. Think about the things in life that stress you out the most. Now write about one of them.

12.3. The Places that Hurt. Describe an event in your life that caused you a considerable amount of pain, hurt, or sadness. Try to write about the event in as much detail as possible and describe how you felt then, and how you feel now as you intentionally relive this event. If it makes it easier, you can write about the experience in a stream-of-consciousness style so that you don't have to worry about how your writing sounds or as a piece of flash writing told from the second person perspective.

If the experience of hurt took place some time ago, you can feel free to write your entry from the perspective of the person you were at the time. Or write a dialogue between your former self and your current self in which your more mature self helps your younger self put the painful experience into some kind of intelligible, meaningful context.

12.4. Things Left Unsaid. Everyone has things that they wish they had taken the time to tell someone close to them but for one reason or another were unable to. Perhaps the opportunity simply never arose or perhaps the person left your life before you had the opportunity to express your feelings. Write a letter to this person expressing those feelings that have been left unsaid. If you prefer, you can write an imaginary dialogue between yourself and this person in which you finally get to express your feelings fully and completely.

12.5. Crazy Emotions. Most of us do everything we can to try to bury painful emotions like fear, guilt, or shame. But bottling up these emotions only makes them more powerful. For this exercise, you are going to confront your inner demons and face them head on:

12.5.1. Fear. Choose one thing in life that you fear greatly and explore what it is about this thing that causes you so much fear. It could be something serious like the possibility of sickness, death, or disfigurement, or it could be something relatively mild, such as a fear of heights, insects, or water.

12.5.2. Guilt and Shame. People typically experience guilt when they have done something harmful to someone else and feel remorse about it. Shame, on the other hand, is usually self-directed, and is usually experienced when we have fallen short of some standard that we set for ourselves. Choose one thing about which you have experienced guilt or shame and write about it, exploring the source of this emotion as deeply as possible. If you prefer you can write this as a poem; or write it as a dialogue between your higher self and the emotion you are examining.

12.6. Expressing Loss. Nothing is more painful in life than the loss of a loved one. Very often, however, people do not have the opportunity to express their grief in a way that allows them to move beyond it. If you have had this kind of loss in your life and have not completely come to terms with it, try writing about your feelings as honestly as you can. If you prefer, you can write an imaginary dialogue between yourself and the person you lost in which you are able to share your feelings directly with them.

12.7. I Don't Want to Write About... The following exercise comes from Sandy Grason's Journalution: "Do you really want to dig deep into your [writing]? Set the timer for ten minutes and write 'I don't want to write about...' at the top of a blank journal page. Then go. You may feel a little twinge in your stomach, or a voice may yell, 'No! No! Don't write that!' You must be fearless, or at least pretend to be, for the next ten minutes. If you are really having a hard time with this, tell yourself that you can always rip it up after you've finished. Asking yourself again and again, 'What do I not want to write about?' will take you deeper and deeper into your fears" (36). Rest assured that, even if you choose not to share this with anyone, it is still a very valuable personal exercise.

12.8. Unsent Letters. Unsent letters are those which we write in order to express thoughts or feeling to a person that are best left unshared for one reason or another. It is actually more of an exercise in self-awareness than it is a method of interpersonal communication.

12.8.1. Think about someone with whom you have unresolved emotional issues. Write this person an unsent letter that expresses your feelings about him or her. If you are having trouble writing the letter, try starting it with a springboard like, "What I've been most afraid to tell you is...." or "I just want you to know how I feel about..." or "[string of expletives]." (Adams, 179).

12.8.2. You can also write an unsent letter to your former self. Write an unsent letter to the child you once were preparing him/her for the difficult experiences that he or she is about to face. Feel free to offer your former self some "mature" advice on how to deal with the pain and suffering that is an inevitable part of life.

12.8.3. Finally, if you want, you can even write an unsent letter to a part of your body about which you feel self-conscious, embarrassed, or resentful (e.g., your crooked nose or your thin legs).

13

The Shadow

In Part Two of this text we examined the persona as the collection of those qualities an individual possesses that he projects to the world in the form of appearance, personality, and beliefs. We also saw that the persona is a kind of mask that the individual wears in his dealings with others. It is the image of ourselves that we present in order to fit in and be accepted by others.

We know that the persona is not the real "self" because it changes as often as necessary to meet the expectations of the outside world. Although the identification of self with persona may make life easier, there is a price we pay for keeping the mask on all the time: deeper dimensions of personality inevitably get covered over and repressed, until there can come a point where we cease to be conscious of them at all.

We saw this very clearly in our examination of the wounded inner child. Our pains, fears, and anxieties are an indelible part of our human identities. But rather than facing these painful aspects of our emotional identity, many people opt instead to repress them. They spend their lives smiling on the outside, while inside they are continually being eaten away by pain and despair.

There is another dark side of our identity that we are even less inclined to acknowledge. This alternative dimension of our personality goes by the name, "the shadow." If the persona presents an idealized image of ourselves to the world, the shadow represents those dark and foreboding aspects of our identity that we would definitely prefer others not to realize we possess. Just like the wounded inner child, the shadow exists in every human being to one degree or another, and demands to be acknowledged, and even embraced. As we shall see, you can try to ignore your shadow, but you definitely do so at your own peril.

What is the Shadow?

In order to fully understand the shadow, let's begin by contrasting it with the persona. In an attempt to fit in and win the approval of others, Carrie Biondi, a 21-year-old college student, creates a persona for herself that fits the image of what she believes others expect of her. If you asked her friends or family to describe Carrie, they would inevitably tell you that she is cheerful, optimistic, kind, loyal, generous, and peaceful. But Carrie knows that the image that she has presented to the world of herself is at least somewhat fictitious. Deep down inside, Carrie is aware that she possesses a great deal of rage, jealousy, selfishness, and resentment. She just can't express these emotions for fear that, if others knew she possessed them, they would reject her.

Carrie, for example, is embittered by the fact that she is not as attractive as some of the other girls she hangs out with, but she often jokes about her appearance to seem congenial. At certain times, however, her resentment comes out in the form of sarcastic barbs directed towards her more attractive friends. If you asked Carrie how she feels towards these friends, she would tell you that she loves them. But, of course, the reason for this is that she too has bought into her own persona. Carrie is so caught up with the image of herself as loyal and devoted that she probably isn't even fully conscious of the dark shadow that lurks inside of her.

So what is this shadow that Carrie is trying so hard to conceal? The shadow is the embodiment of deep-rooted, unresolved destructiveness, aggression, hatred, and hostility. It contains all of our most violent and destructive primal urges—urges that are so powerful and unsettling that most people would prefer to pretend that they don't exist at all. As William Miller puts it:

> The shadow is like a foreign personality—a primitive, instinctive, animalistic kind of being. It is the collection of uncivilized desires and feelings that simply have no place in our cultured society. The shadow is everything we don't want to be. Or rather it is perhaps everything we would *like* to be but don't dare. The shadow is everything we don't want others to know about us. It is everything we don't even want to know about ourselves and have thus conveniently "forgotten" through denial and repression (23).

Sounds pretty unpleasant, doesn't it? No wonder so many people do all they can to forget they even have a shadow.   But repressing the shadow, as we shall see, is a dubious strategy for dealing with our dark, turbulent emotions.

Befriending Your Shadow

Many of us have grown up in families where expressions of emotions such as anger were strongly discouraged. A child raised in this kind of family learns to develop a persona that masks his anger. He will quickly figure out that he should smile and be pleasant around others if he wants to win their approval and avoid frowning or expressing his frustrations.

These dark emotions may be repressed for a time, but they are certainly not eliminated. They become the building blocks of the shadow. In repressing these emotions, we actually give them more power than they might otherwise have. As the psychologist Karl Jung writes, "Unfortunately there can be no doubt that man is, on the whole, less good than he imagines himself or wants to be. Everyone carries a shadow, and the less it is embodied in the individual's conscious life, the blacker and denser it is." (*Collected Works*, Vol. 11, 131).

The shadow also has a nasty habit of surfacing when we least expect it. In general, the greater the degree of repression, the greater the amount of damage an unleashed shadow can cause. We've all heard cases of seemingly mild-mannered people who suddenly explode in rage because of some completely insignificant slight. The failure to come to terms with emotions like anger often means that such emotions take on a life of their own that we are unable to control.

The strategy of trying to ignore the shadow also has the potential to cause tremendous harm to our emotional and physical health. In fact, health studies have recently shown that not expressing one's anger and frustration can lead to heart-related health issues later on in life. Believe it or not, you can actually drop dead from trying to repress your shadow!

So if repression is not a viable option for dealing with the shadow— and, in fact, does little more than throw fuel onto the fire of our destructive urges—how are we to deal with our shadows? The answer, as Robert Johnson writes is to come to learn to acknowledge our shadows and learn to deal with them: "No one can be anything but a partial being, ravaged by doubt and loneliness, unless he has close contact with his shadow. Assimilating one's shadow is the art of catching up on those facts of life that have not been lived out adequately."

This in no way means that we should give full vent to our destructive urges, which is equally unproductive and can lead to horrible consequences.

The key to a healthy emotional life is to achieve some kind of balance between repressing violent emotions and simply giving in to them. As much as possible we want to be mindful of all of our emotional states, to understand how they affect us, and what they say about who we are as human beings.

This is certainly not a new concept. In fact, more than 2,500 years ago, the Buddha developed a method for achieving a heightened state of awareness about these kinds of emotional states. The method that he developed has come to be known in modern times as mindfulness practice. The Buddha believed that we could achieve a state of mindfulness about many different aspects of our lives—what the body is feeling, our thoughts, our fantasies. He also believed that it was possible to achieve full mindfulness of emotional states, including those that are destructive if acted upon.

Take the following situation, for example:

You are sitting in the living room watching TV and your mother comes in and begins to berate you for forgetting to keep a promise you made to take out the garbage. As is typically the case in such encounters, you begin to get angry with your mother for bothering you when you are trying to unwind after a long and difficult day at school. How do you respond to this situation? You could try repressing your anger, but that will only lead to even more pent up frustration. Or you could explode at your mother, but that probably will only cause you greater guilt and more problems later on.

The alternative approach is to turn your attention to the emotions that you are experiencing at the moment your mother is harping at you. Study the emotions that surface intensely. Allow yourself to feel the emotion completely and study how it affects your body (e.g., racing heart, clammy hands, rapid respiration). Don't judge the emotions that you are experiencing as good or bad, because they are actually neither in themselves. They just are. Accept that.

If you've done this, what would your reaction be towards your mother? Most likely you would be able to express your frustrations at how you are being treated without responding in anger. Depending upon your mother's personality, this, in turn, might lead her to respond far differently than if you had reacted to her in rage. Your shadow would be acknowledged, but it would relinquish all of its power over you. In a sense, you would have made "friends with your shadow."

The basic idea of mindfulness practice, as is evident in the above illustration, is to sit with dark emotions for a while, rather than acting upon them immediately, to try to view them objectively, and observe with as much detachment as possible how these emotions affect your body, your mind, and your future actions.

The Shadow and Creativity

You might be tempted to believe that, at best, since the shadow is an integral part of your personality, it has to be accepted because there really isn't any other choice. You can't get rid of your deep, dark emotions, so you just have to learn to deal with them. Right?

While it's true that the inner turmoil caused by your shadow is rarely pleasant, this in no way means that having a shadow lurking inside you is all bad. In fact, without the existence of both a wounded inner child and a shadow, you would probably be little more than a flat, one-dimensional excuse for a human being. Think about the few people you might know who are always cheerful, never sad or upset about anything, who never get enraged or frustrated by life. How interesting are these people? Without the inner turmoil created by the presence of the shadow there would be no reason to grow as a human being, your emotions would never have the opportunity to develop, and real psychological maturity would probably be impossible.

Even more important for our purposes, it's the shadow that makes the creation really profound works of art possible. As Carl Jung wrote, "In spite of its function as a reservoir for human darkness—or perhaps because of this—the shadow is the seat of creativity." Many—and perhaps even most—great works of art emerge from the dark side of an artist's personality. If an artist had no dark side, the work that he or she would produce would probably be insipid. Conflict itself is the very stuff out of which great works of art are created. Try to imagine a film, a novel, or a play in which there is no conflict at all and in which all of the main characters are deliriously happy all the time. Would you really want to read or watch that kind of work?

The process whereby violent and destructive impulses are channeled into something more productive is known as "sublimation." During the process of sublimation, destructive urges are transformed into something higher and more socially redeeming. Instead of getting drunk or punching someone out when these impulses emerge, the act of sublimation enables us to transfer the energy away from the destructive act towards something more creative.

Gaining access to the shadow as a mine for creativity necessitates getting beyond your need to produce what other people like or approve of and to get beyond what you think you should be writing. As Kim Addonizio and Dorianne Lax write in *The Poet's Companion,* being willing to tap into your shadow means:

> going into territory that may be labeled "forbidden," or that may

be personally difficult. It is important not to censor yourself. Give yourself permission to explore wherever the writing takes you. Of course, this kind of writing—going towards that which is hardest to speak of...takes a certain amount of courage. Your normal, denying self doesn't want to deal with those things. But sometimes writing may be the only place you can express them. There's a great feeling of relief and catharsis when you manage to get something that's been buried or hidden out onto the page. And such a process, whether or not it eventually results in a poem, helps to integrate that part of the self (57-58).

Nobody ever said that getting in touch with your shadow would be easy or pleasant. But, if you have the courage to face the darkness that lies inside you, you may just discover that tapping into your shadow-side can prove beneficial. It can allow you to explore thoughts, feelings, and memories that you've probably worked extremely hard to repress, and, in doing so, can help you come to terms with them. And, if you are really courageous, you might even be able to use what emerges from the exploration of your shadow to create something really incredible—something that captures an essential part of who you are.

For Reflection

We've seen that it takes a great deal of practice to rest comfortably with the often disturbing emotions that arise when we confront our shadows. Most people either instinctively run away in horror or get sucked in by the drama of these emotions. To be able to face our dark emotions without giving into them is a skill that is extremely difficult to master.

To this end, think about a time when you experienced a destructive emotion such as anger, envy, jealousy, or hatred, and reflect upon the following:

1. What were the specific circumstances that gave rise to this dark emotion?

2. What were you experiencing as you went through this state (Try as much as possible to relive this experience. Don't just recall it; feel it inside you).

3. How does it feel right now to relive this experience?

Express Yourself

As we have seen there is a definite psychological benefit to allowing your shadow to expose itself in constructive and creative ways. The writing exercises in this chapter, as with those in the previous chapter on the wounded inner child, might prove difficult for some people. If you find yourself feeling overwhelmed as you try to do some of these exercises, feel free to skip them and work on something else for the time being. You may find that at some other point in this program, you feel the urge to explore your shadow and are able to tackle some of the dark feelings that are buried inside all of us. That's perfectly fine too. Although you should try to move beyond your comfort zone in writing, exactly how and when you do this is your call.

Here are just a few exercises that we have found conducive to making friends with your shadow:

13.1. Counterpoint. Take some thing or some act that you find disgusting, horrible, offensive, or frightening. Write about it as though you loved it. Go as far as you can in singing its praises. If you want, you can write a love poem about it.

13.2. Rant-o-Mania. Write the foulest rant you can about someone or something that you truly hate. Feel free to let yourself go with this exercise, using stream-of-consciousness writing and dredging up as many mean vicious vile worlds and images as you can to write about this person or thing. If you prefer you can write an unsent letter of pure unadulterated hatred towards someone who did you wrong or who you intensely dislike for whatever reason. Once again, however, don't hold any of your venom back.

13.3. The Belly of the Beast. Tap into the shadow that lies within you. What violent, destructive urges do you potentially possess that could create havoc if left uncheck? Explore these urges and write about them in prose, poetry or dialogue form.

13.4. The Horror, The Horror. What is the most horrific thing you can image in life? Write a piece of flash fiction or non-fiction that explores this horror in all its dimensions.

13.5. Nightmare. Write about a recent nightmare you had that was particularly frightening. If you prefer you can make up your own imaginary nightmare.

13.6. Dialogue between your inner angel and demon. Each of us has an angel and a demon lurking inside of us. Create a imaginary dialogue between yours between yours exploring the light and dark dimensions of your own personality.

13.7. This is The End. Imagine your own death scene, funeral, or burial. Now describe one of these events in detail, using all of your imaginative powers. If you prefer, you can write a story about this event.

14

The Fantastic Self

By now you must be thinking that the real you—the you that you experience when you plumb the depths of your inner being—must be one seriously sick and disturbed creature. For the past two weeks, you've been exploring the psychic pain, turmoil, anxiety, rage, and anguish that we all possess, but which most of us choose to keep under cover. If, after two weeks of this dark exploration, you feel like you are about to go out of you mind, I have some good news for you: things brighten up considerably from this point onward.

There are certainly those who tend to dwell on the dark side of their nature. They usually wind up dressed in black and fantasizing about death (their own or others). While I certainly believe that this dimension of the human psyche exists in just about everyone to one degree or another, I also know for a fact that in the deepest level of our being, there exists much more than the wounded child and the shadow. I know this because there have been men and women throughout the course of human history who have been able to transcend the darkness within themselves and tap into more luminescent dimensions of their spirits for creative purposes.

The first of these alternative dimensions that I would like to explore has been underappreciated by psychologists both as a source of self-actualization and as a dynamic font of creative inspiration. For lack of a better term, we can call this dimension of your identity the "fantastic self."

To get some idea of what this fantastic self is like, we can turn to the writing of Carlos Melendez, an art major, who is considered by family and friends as being a bit "unconventional" to say the least. Here's what Carlos wrote when he was asked to write as candidly as possible about his inner self:

> *I'm a real freak—no doubt about it. In terms of appearance, people think I'm strange enough with my tattoos, piercings, and long hair. But if they knew what was inside of me, they'd definitely run away as fast as they could.*
>
> *I guess I've never been a slave to "normal" ideas about the right way to behave or think. Normal for me is like death. How can you be alive if you are living or thinking exactly like everyone else?*
>
> *In my mind there is always a flood of images going on at any moment. Some of them are dark, for sure, but most are just strange and freaky: bright, pulsating lights in psychedelic colors, images of pale, death-like women reaching out to me, strange animals with saucer-sized eyes and mouths filled with razor-sharp teeth, endless dark hallways with doors opening and closing on every side, leading to vast fields of bright flowers and rolling hills, Christ crucified on the cross while Wall Street types talk on their cell-phones, oblivious to his suffering.*
>
> *These sorts of images are always working their way into my sketches and paintings. I may not be as skillful a painter as some of my classmates, but my art is definitely much more original and interesting. They are always thinking about what their professors want them to paint, but I always just paint what's inside of me— what I call my inner freak. And, believe me, that's never going to be boring!*

What Carlos possesses to an extraordinary degree is what he refers to as his "inner freak," but which might better be capture by the name "the fantastic self." The roots of the word "fantastic" actually come from the Greek *phantastikos* which means "to be able to imagine" and the French *fantastique*, which means "existing only in the imagination." Also closely associated with this term is the noun "phantasm," which can be defined as "a vision of something that has no physical or objective reality."

So the fantastic self (or the phantastic self, to be more precise) is that inner dimension of the human person that is not bound by objective reality—reality, in other words, as it exists "out there," as captured by the senses. And, since the fantastic is not limited by what is taken in through sense perception, it's able to achieve the most extraordinary flights of fancy that imagination itself is capable of. What I refer to, then, as the fantastic self can best be described as the wild, spontaneous, uninhibited, sometimes freaky, always unconventional aspect of the human identity that surfaces when the individual gives free reign to his imagination and allows it to begin to shape his understanding of the world around him and his place within it. Imagination, then, plays a central role in determining whether our fantastic selves are going to be unleashed or whether they will remain buried unborn within us.

The Fantastic Self and the Imagination

We might begin by asking what the imagination is, anyway? The word imagination itself comes from the Latin "*imago*," meaning image. Imagination can be understood, therefore, as the process whereby one forms images in the mind. But not just any sort of images, since mental images can also be formed during normal acts of sensation. I perceive a tree, for example, and later on, while I am in my room, form a fairly exact mental image of that same tree in my mind for a topographical survey I have to perform. But that's really not what imagination is about, now is it?

Imagination involves the creation of new images in the mind that have not previously been experienced or which have been experienced only partially or in different combinations. The ancient Greeks, for example, came up with the idea of the centaur. In doing so, they were able to combine two fairly common images in their minds—the human being and the horse. There is nothing imaginative about either of these alone, but when you combine these two images, you have something that does not and has never existed in reality—the centaur. This is where imagination begins.

The other thing to keep in mind about imaginative thinking—as opposed to scientific thinking—is that there is nothing necessarily practical about the images, concepts and ideas produced as a result of using our imaginations. Whereas science always aims at what is useful or beneficial, the imagination is not limited at all by such mundane concerns. We allow our imaginations to run wild, because it is pleasant to do so, and any other consideration is secondary at best. To ask a young child who is making up some fabulous story, for example, what the function or purpose such story-telling is would be met by a look of incomprehension on the part of the child. Children tell stories (or make up games or pretend to be other people or create silly songs) because it is fun to do so, and usually for no other reason.

Finally, we've all heard it said time and again that it is important for people in just about every field to learn to "think outside the box." In the 1990s Apple Computers even had a campaign that encouraged the purchasers of its computers to "think different." But what exactly does it mean to "think outside the box" or "think different" anyway? Who exactly are we supposed to be thinking differently from? What are we supposed to be thinking differently than?

Most men and women have a natural tendency to conform their ideas to those of the status quo. This sort of thinking is convergent, since the aim is arrive at some kind of synthesis of thought. There's nothing wrong with this sort of thinking per se, but it is hardly going to achieve brilliant flights of intellectual fancy achieved by truly visionary thinkers or artists like Leonardo Da Vinci or Albert Einstein. That kind of revolutionary way of looking at the world requires breaking away from the status quo and engaging in what I would call divergent or discordant thinking (as opposed to convergent or consensus thinking). And it's imagination that enables us to think in this divergent sort of way—to think different, in other words. As the poet Wallace Stevens once put it, imagination is "the power that enables us to perceive the normal in the abnormal, the opposite of chaos in chaos."

Systematic Derangement

It seems, then, that society benefits greatly when the kind of divergent, imaginative thinking that we've described is allowed to flourish. And, if we encouraged people to develop the potential of their fantastic selves, the results could potentially be extraordinary. So the question becomes, is there a way in which the true potentials of our fantastic selves can become unleashed and used as a springboard for personal and creative liberation?

In *The Doors of Perception*, Aldous Huxley once famously wrote: "If the doors of perception were cleansed every thing would appear to man as it is, infinite. For man has closed himself up, till he sees all things through narrow chinks of his cavern." In the same work, Huxley expressed the goal of mankind as to be "shaken out of the ruts of ordinary perception, to be shown for a few timeless hours the outer and inner world, not as they appear to an animal obsessed with survival or to a human being obsessed with words and notions, but as they are apprehended, directly and unconditionally, by Mind at Large."

Huxley's view is that we human beings have allowed ourselves to view the world through the narrow and constricting prism of ordinary perception. In *The Doors of Perception*, he posits that if we could but "cleanse" our way of looking at the world—to get beyond, in other words, the tyranny of our scientific, pragmatic ways of understanding reality—new possibilities that are virtually limitless would open themselves up to us. The full potentials of our fantastic selves, in other words, would inevitably be unleashed.

So how exactly does one go about liberating his or her mind from its ordinary, mundane forms of perception? Actually, this has been a question that has intrigued artists and writers for most of the 20th century, but particularly during the 1950s and 60s in the United States, when a new consciousness was developing in the country and young people in particular were searching for ways to break beyond the conformist sensibilities of their parents' generations. The figure that many of these iconoclastic visionaries looked to in particular was a young poet with a checkered past and some rather strange ideas about artistic liberation—the 19th century French bad-boy, Arthur Rimbaud.

Born in 1854 in the small French town of Charleville, Rimbaud had already begun winning awards for his writing by the age of 13. Attempting to flee the sterile conformism of his home life, he went to Paris and began a torrid affair with the poet Paul Verlaine, which ended badly for both of them. In 1873, he wrote his most famous work, *A Season in Hell* (*Une Saison en Enfer*), which had an enormous impact on the direction of modern poetry. By the age of 19, Rimbaud stopped writing poetry completely and left for Africa as a colonial tradesman. In 1891 he developed a cancerous growth in his leg; the leg was amputated, but the cancer continued to spread, and he died at the age of 37.

In letters that Rimbaud wrote when he was still only a teenager, he outlined his vision for the true poet:

> Right now, I'm beshitting myself as much as possible. Why? I want to be a poet, and I'm working to turn myself into a *seer*: you won't understand at all, and it's unlikely that I'll be able to explain it to you. It has to do with making your way towards the unknown by a *derangement of all the senses*. The suffering is tremendous, but one must bear up against it, to be born a poet, and I know that's what I am (365).

> The Poet makes himself into a *seer* by a long, involved and logical *derangement of all the senses*. Every kind of love, of suffering, of madness; he searches himself; he exhausts every possible poison so that only one essence remains. He undergoes unspeakable tortures that require complete faith and superhuman strength, rendering him the ultimate Invalid among men, the master criminal, the first among the damned—the supreme Savant! For

he arrives at the unknown! For, unlike everyone else, he has developed an already rich soul. He arrives at the unknown, and when, bewildered, he ends up losing his understanding of his visions, he has, at least, seen them! It doesn't matter if these leaps into the unknwn kill him: other awful workers will follow him; they'll start at the horizons where the other has fallen (367-368).

As I mentioned, Rimbaud inspired many of his own contemporaries, but it was not until the 1950s, when he was "discovered" by Beat Generation writers like Jack Kerouac, William Burroughs, and Alan Ginsberg that Rimbaud's vision truly began to take hold.

In particular Rimbaud's view that true vision is attained by the artist though "a long…and systematic derangement of the senses" (*dérèglement raisonné de tous les sens*) would have an enormous role to play in the art, music, and culture of the Beats and the Counterculture. For Rimbaud, this disorganization took the form of wild evenings drinking absinthe and smoking hashish to excess and engaging in outrageous behavior that scandalized Parisian society. When the Beat writers encountered Rimbaud during their years at Columbia University they too attempted systematic derangement through excessive alcohol consumption, experimentation with narcotics, and anti-social forms of behavior (cohabitation, homosexual activity, the celebration of the criminal, the junkie, and in general all outcasts of society).

Later in the 1960s, Rimbaud provided the inspiration for the founding members of the Counterculture, who saw LSD as a way of achieving Huxley's cleansing of the doors of perception. Individuals as diverse as Timothy Leary (a Harvard psychologist), Richard Alpert (later to become Hindu mystic Ram Dass), Huston Smith (theologian and author of The Religions of Man), and Andrew Weil (natural health guru) would unite to form the Harvard Psychadelic club, the aim of which was to use drugs like LSD to achieve personal and spiritual liberation.

There's no doubt that some of the greatest achievements of 1960s Counterculture—in particular the wild, psychedelic music of the period—were fueled by the use of LSD. Bob Dylan, The Beatles, The Greatful Dead, The Doors, and Jefferson Airplane wrote some of their most original music while under the influence of the drug. Unfortunately, LSD proved to be a gateway drug that lead to the deaths of some of the brightest stars of the sixties music scene—most notably, Janis Joplin, Jim Morrison, and Jimmy Hendrix—and to serious rehab issues for many others.

The heavy toll that drug use took on young people during the 1960s would make the lifestyles of the Counterculture—and to a lesser extent the Beat Generation—seem somehow illegitimate as a result. But what exactly was the goal of those admittedly unconventional lifestyles? It was nothing other than the desire to liberate oneself from the tyranny of conformism, to explore one's deeper potential as a human being, and to allow one's innate and unique creative potential to reveal itself as a result. To the extent that human beings have fantastic selves buried within them, it seems evident that at least some members of the Beat Generation of the 1950s and the Counterculture of the 1960s were extraordinarily successful in unleashing them and produced wild, uninhibited, often surrealistic creative work as a result.

Controlled Psychic Disorientation

If Rimbaud was correct, and the systematic derangement of the senses is one way to allow the full potential of our fantastic selves to be released, then can the same result be achieved without having to resort to the kind of dangerous and destructive practices that did in many prominent members of the 60s counterculture? The crippling disease of conformism in our society, however, is so strong that it needs to be overcome with equally potent medicine. If we want to unleash our fantastic selves, then we need to compel the mind to break free of its natural tendencies to view the world in sterile and conformists ways.

This is definitely not an easy process, which is probably why so few people succeed in getting in touch with their fantastic selves. It actually takes a commitment to change one's life almost completely in order to lay ground that is fertile for the wild, spontaneous, unconventional aspects of one's identity to emerge.

To aid you in this grand process, try experimenting with some or all of the following recommendations:

1. *Seek out unconventional people to use as your life guides.* From our teenage years on most of us gravitate towards certain individuals who serve as models for how we would like to behave. Unfortunately, most of us seek out individuals who conform to society's expectations of what is cool or appropriate (In other words, our role models are usually quite boring and conventional people). But there are some seriously strange, provocative, non-conformist individuals out there who have already tapped into their own fantastic selves. You won't find these sorts of people at the places you usually frequent—the trendy bar or dance club, the shopping mall, or the local Starbucks. You've got to go to the kinds of places where serious artists, musicians, poets, outcasts, and freaks hang out, and that tends to vary from city to city.

But once you find where the "different ones" dwell and you start to get to know them, you'll discover just how much they have to offer you (at least compared to the jocks, party girls, and shopping queens that you might formerly have looked up to). These will typically be the kind of people that your mother warned you against when she advised you to seek out "decent friends". They'll probably dress poorly, smell bad, and often act in socially inappropriate ways...but they will always be a source for endless inspiration.

2. *Engage in experiences that can nurture your fantastic self.* This might include travel to exotic places, spending time alone in nature, exploring grungy urban settings, going to see experimental performances, hanging out at contemporary art museums or galleries, or anything else that might stimulate your imagination. Just try to get out of your usual environment now and then, and intentionally put yourself in settings that are unfamiliar or which might even make you feel uncomfortable. Above all else, if you live in middle class suburbia, find time to escape from it as often as possible, since the suburban milieu is the kiss of death for the soul.

3. *Try on different roles for yourself (and recognize that you are not limited by any of the roles that you play).* You don't have to be you all the time. You can be anyone you want to be. Pretend to be someone else for a while. The more bizarre or outrageous the persona you create for yourself, the better. Steep yourself in the being of the fantastic identity you create, and walk in his or her shoes for a while. Then discard this imaginary identity and try on a new one. You'd be surprised at how liberating it can be to take on a new identity, even for a little while—especially if that identity is completely different from your own.

4. *Experiment with new, untried, eclectic modes of self-expression.* Whatever your prefered mode of creative expression is—writing, painting, photography, film-making, etc.—there comes a point where you are probably just coasting along doing what you've always done and sticking with what is comfortable and safe for you. But the fantastic self needs challenges to thrive, and this means shaking things up precisely at the moment when you are most certain about your artistic direction in life. Try intentionally doing bad, strange, tasteless, or even shocking work, just to make sure that you don't fall into a rut. Don't worry at all about what people will think of your work; in fact, go out of your way to create art that will be alienating to as many people as possible. Again, you'll probably find this sort of practice to be incredibly liberating.

5. *...and above all else, begin to change your fundamental attitude towards your own life.* In order to provide truly fertile ground for the fantastic self to thrive, you got to avoid thinking of yourself as a static entity—a specific and unchanging being trapped in a particular place and time—and start thinking of yourself as a pure, unadulterated possibility

or potentiality. Your entire life must be viewed as one grand experiment in self-discovery, and this means you've got to be willing to evolve and change all the time. Remember: there is no essential, permenanently enduring you; there is only an endless stream of thoughts, feelings, and sensations that are not connected to any thinker, feeler, sensor. You are whatever you choose to be in life, and you are not limited by anything other than your own self-limiting self-conception.

These five recommendations probably require a lifetime of practice and experimentation. I certainly don't expect you to discover your fantastic self over night. All you need to do is try to stretch yourself gently and move slowly in the direction of adopting non-conformist sensibilities in your life. To the extent that you can even begin to see that you have choices in life and are not a slave to the prevailing bourgeois notions of good and bad, beautiful and ugly, and true and false, to that extent will you give some much-needed wiggle room for your poor underappreciated fantastic self to emerge.

For Reflection

This exercise is based upon one found in Julia Cameron's *The Artists Way* (100-101).

What would you like to try that you are not allowed to do? What would you like to try if you didn't have to worry about people thinking that you were irresponsible, reckless, crazy, or selfish:

-

-

-

-

-

Cameron says that if your list is filled with things that are exciting or even crazy, then you're on the right tack. If, upon reviewing your list, however, you find that it is too safe or conventional, then force yourself to add at least one more item to the list that is at least borderline wacky.

Express Yourself

It's now time to tap into your fantastic self. Find the wild, spontaneous, uninhibited, freaky being inside yourself and let this shine through in your writing this week.

14.1. Induced Psychosis. Imagine that you've gone completely and totally insane and your perceptions of reality are completely out of sync from what most people experience. Put yourself in that mindset and then write a piece the way an insane person would. Success in writing this piece is measured by how far you can take your writing away from what is "normal."

14.2. Record a Dream. The writer Jack Kerouac wrote an entire book just of his dreams. Dreams—especially recurring dreams—provide fascinating information about your inner life. Jungian psychologists in particular believe that dreams provide the key to your subconscious. Kathleen Adams argues that dreams provide both mundane and profound purposes:

> Some dreams function as a sort of inner secretary, reminding you of tasks left uncompleted or real-life events that may have slipped your conscious mind...Other dreams can point you down a path of inner awareness and growth. Still others can help clarify difficulties, relationships, parts of yourself that are clamoring for attention. And sometimes dreams can lead to life-changing decisions (191-192).

Because dreams can be so elusive, in order to capture them in their full vividness, you probably will need to keep a notebook and pen by your bed. In the morning, as soon as you've awakened, write down as much as you can remember of your dreams, even if is just an image or scene, a mood or a feeling.

If you are lucky enough to awaken from a dream in the middle of the night, write it down immediately. Don't worry about writing in proper English; just get as many of the details down as possible.

You have two options with respect to your writing: The first is simply to keep a dream log, recording anything you can remember about your dreams each morning for a set period (three days, a week). Just jot down whatever you can remember in stream-of-consciousness style.

If you have a dream or a nightmare that you can recall vividly, the second option would be to write about the dream in detail, trying to capture everything you can about the dream.

14.3.   Guided Imagery. Read the following passage and then complete it as your own personal fairy tale:

> Imagine that you are on a special journey through a magical kingdom. You are walking through a dense forest. As you leave the forest, you suddenly see a castle in the distance a castle. You approach the castle hesitantly, because you don't know what's inside. The doors of the castle are closed. They are huge, but you push with all your strength and they gradually begin to open.

Describe what you see and experience, who you meet, and what you learn, as you walk through the castle. Feel free to let your imagination run wild.

14.4.   Fantastic Flash Fiction. Try writing a few pieces of short fantastic flash fiction. Make them no more than one or two paragraphs and try to stretch the boundaries of how strange you can make them sound...in fact, the weirder the better! Try to write several of these kinds of strange short pieces, challenging yourself to get more and more freaky with each one.

14.5. Fantasy Drama. Try writing an intentionally weird or strange dramatic scene. See just how bizarre you can be in your writing. Remember, the more bizarre, the better.

14.6.   Alternate Universe. Create a piece of flash fiction describing a strange incident that happened to an unsuspecting individual (this could be yourself) in an alternative universe. This could be a dream world, a parallel universe, or another planet.

14.7. Cut-Outs. Take an old magazine or newspaper and cut out words, phrases and sentences that strike your fancy from different sections of the publication. Put these cut-outs together on a table and type out the resulting text.

15

The Transcendent Self

We are coming to the end of our Creative Self program. For 15 weeks you put an incredibly bright spotlight on yourself, exploring virtually every conceivable dimension of what it means to be a human person. At times you probably didn't like what you experienced very much—for instance, having to stare at yourself in the mirror or confronting your inner psychic wounds and darkest demons. On the other hand, perhaps your explorations during the past 15 weeks have given you a newfound appreciation for just how unique, interesting, and complex a person you actually are! Are you beginning to understand by now that there is only one you in the entire world, and another person exactly like you will never come along again in human history? If you've even come close to appreciating that insight, that's quite an achievement in and of itself.

Now, in the final week of our program, we are going to try to destroy any remaining preconceptions you may have about your life and who you are as a person. We know from our study of the persona that you are often not what you appear to others to be. And we know from looking at the wounded child and the shadow that the deepest dimensions of who you are as human beings is often far different from —and much darker than—the image that you typically present to the world.

But when we get to the deepest and most profound aspect of your human identity—which we will call the transcendent self—you probably couldn't even begin to imagine just how amazingly awesome you actually are, or fathom your infinite potentiality as a being who, as we are going to see, has the ability to transcend the very limitations of human identity itself.

The Brute Facts of Life

Let's start our exploration of the transcendent self by looking at the human condition in as stark and unromantic a light as possible. If we look objectively at a human life, there are certain brute facts about existence that seem to apply to everyone:

(YOUR NAME)'S STORY

1. You were born into this life with no control over where you were born, to whom you were born, or in what social and economic conditions you were born. You couldn't decide to stay in the womb rather than being thrust out into the world naked and screaming, and once you were born, you pretty much were handed a dealt deck in terms of your genetic make-up and your environment. If you were very lucky, you weren't born in a war zone or to abusive parents or with a life-threatening disability or mentally incapacitated.

2. For approximately 18-25 years of your life, you grew physically and developed, to a greater or lesser degree, the intellectual, psychological, and social skills needed to navigate your way through life and find your place within human society.

3. For much of the rest of your life, you put the skills you learned to use working in some kind of job—in all likelihood, one that you didn't enjoy very much or that didn't pay you the kind of salary that you thought you deserved. The money that you earned from working, however, enabled you eventually to leave your parent's home and pay for those items necessary for survival (food, clothing, housing) and those that contribute to human felicity (cars, Iphones, designer handbags, etc,).

4. Like all animals, you have a built-in desire to procreate and to spread your gene pool as widely as possible to ensure the survival of the species. If conditions were right, you may have found a suitable partner with whom to produce offspring. You would then spend the most productive years of your mid-life providing for those offspring, attempting to ensure their survival into adulthood,

and training them—with greater or lesser success—to become autonomous individuals in their own right.

5. If you were lucky, you didn't die accidentally, perish from a disease, or be killed, and made it into old age. At that point your body began to break down, you got sick, you suffered physically (and perhaps emotionally as well) and eventually died. Within moments after your death, your body began to decompose, and within a few years, almost nothing was left of you at all.

6. Within one or two generations of your death, you were forgotten by every other human being on the planet (unless you were one of the ridiculously small percentage of human beings who were skillful or lucky enough to make an impact on human history, in which case, you might be remembered a bit longer). Your grandchildren will probably only have fleeting memories of you and their children will only know who you were through dusty, old photographs that have been left behind (if they haven't already been tossed away by a careless descendant, that is).

7. With a relatively short amount of time—planetarily speaking—humanity itself will be destroyed through some kind of global cataclysm or pandemic and nothing will remain of our species. At some point in time a new species may evolve from the bugs that have managed to survive, but this species will probably have little or nothing in common with our own. Eventually, the planet, and even the universe itself, will simply cease to exist, and all that will remain will be the infinite void.

These are the basic facts about the human condition. These are not the facts about the existence of some people; they are facts that apply to everyone equally, no matter how privileged or fortunate a person's life may appear on the surface. To be more specific, this is YOUR story.

Reflection

Do you think that any of the facts stated in the above narrative don't apply to you? If so, which ones? How does reading this narrative make you feel about your human life?

There are different ways that people choose to respond to these brute facts about human existence—and in particular the objective truth that we will eventually die and be completely forgotten and that eventually everything that exists now as we know it will also disappear into cosmic oblivion.

The completely unreflective person, who lives for the moment and refuses to think about unpleasant subjects like death, seems to have some advantage here over his more introspective counterpart. He can block out all thoughts about personal oblivion as he swills his cheap beer and focuses on life's immediate pleasure (what the ancient Romans would call "bread and circuses"). But even the most unreflective person eventually will be confronted by the stark fact of his own finitude in the form of the physical pain, suffering, and death that is inevitable in life. In some ways, his completely unconscious mode of existing will leave him totally unprepared to face the end of his existence and, as a result, he will likely experience far more fear and depression than a more introspective person might.

On the opposite end of the spectrum is the existential-type of person, who thinks about these issues all the time and whose whole life is filled with anxiety and despair. If you've ever watched a Woody Allen film, you know exactly what this type of person is like. He tends to be fairly intellectual, given to obsessing over the minutest aspects of the human condition and finding human existence lacking.

For the existentialist, human existence is characterized by absurdity— the idea that there is no ultimate meaning or purpose to the world or to our lives. Really horrible and tragic things happen to really good people (shit happens) and basically there is not much we can do about it. The existentialist understands that, if there is to be any real meaning in life, he has to create it for himself. But the act for having to serve as his own supreme being, with all the responsibility that involves, fills the heart of the existentialist with anxiety, despair, and dread (otherwise referred to as existential angst). All this leads Albert Camus, a notable 20th century existentialist, to claim that there really is only one true philosophical problem—that of suicide. Keep living, in other words, in the face of the absurdity of life, or end your life totally and be done with it. Those are really the only two viable options an existentialist has.

What the unreflective person and the existentialist have in common is recognition of the fundamental banality of the human condition. We're born, we live, we suffer, we die, and ultimately we are forgotten. The unreflective individual tries to run from this truth by drowning himself in distracting pleasures (To quote a famous Peggy Lee song from the 1960s: "Is that all there is, my friends. Break out the booze and have a ball, if that's all there is."). The existentialist doesn't take this easy way out, but his life is no less bleak. In the end all he has is his despair and the troubling thoughts of whether human life is all worth it in the end.

But are these really our only two options in life?

Things Ain't What They Appear to Be

A third option does indeed present itself when we consider what to do with the basic facts of human life as I've presented them above. This third option is a bit trickier than the first two, because it basically involves disputing what seems to be a self-evident fact about human experience—that things are as they appear to be. But what if everything we think is real about the world we inhabit is actually more like a fiction than a reality? We'd then have to try, to the best of our abilities, to peer beyond the fictional world that we think actually exists the way that we perceive it and try to uncover reality as it ACTUALLY exists.

If this seems like the plotline of some kind of science fiction or fantasy film—in fact, it is the basis for the films *The Matrix* and *Inception*—there have been a number of great thinkers throughout the centuries who have posited just this very fact about the way we perceive the world around us and our place in it.

For example, in his myth of the cave, the Greek philosopher, Plato, presents an allegory that represents what he believes to be the "really real" world, as opposed to the illusionary world that we think exists. To put this allegory briefly, Plato has us imagine an underground cave, in which a group of prisoners are chained and able to see only what is in front of them. Behind the prisoners is a fire in front of which men walk carrying objects that cast shadows on the walls of the cave. Since all they've been exposed to are these images, the prisoners naturally come to think that the shadows on the wall are in fact reality. But in a dramatic twist, Plato has one of the prisoners escape from the darkness of the cave. At first, he is blinded by the bright light of the sun, but after his eyes adjust he comes to realize that what he is experiencing outside the cave is reality and all he thought was real was mere illusion. Feeling pity on his fellow prisoners, he goes back into the cave to try to liberate them. In the end, the prisoners kill the one who is trying to free them, so convinced are they that the shadows they experience inside the cave are the only true reality.

One could spend an entire book trying to peel apart the layers of this allegory, but for our purposes what Plato is suggesting is that we are the prisoners that he describes in his myth, who think that the images they experience inside the cave are reality, when in fact they are anything but. The real world, Plato argues, is the world that exists outside the cave, and if we could just train our minds properly—like the prisoner who escapes from his bondage—we too would be able to see the reality as it truly is and be liberated from our lives of delusion. The real world for Plato is not the world that the senses perceive—that's the deception of the cave—but rather the world of pure ideas that transcends the material world. According to

Plato, although we perceive a physical world with separate entities doing their thing, on a much deeper level, there is only Being, a transcendent reality in which all things participate.

Even before Plato was thinking about his cave, there were a group of spiritual thinkers in India who had similar ideas about reality. These ideas are expressed in their purest form in the great Hindu classics, *The Upanishads* and are part of the spiritual tradition known as Vedanta. The insight that these spiritual writers had was that reality was really ONE; we are all part, they believe, of the great cosmic spirit, also known as Brahman or God. The problem is that our minds create the illusion that there is multiplicity instead of unity. We perceive ourselves as separate from the world around us and others (the illusion of "I," "me," and "mine") when in actuality there is only oneness. This illusion of separateness and multiplicity is what those in the Vedantic tradition refer to as Maya. Only by purifying one's consciousness can one peer beyond the veil of deception created by Maya and once again recognize one's own basic unity with all of reality.

While these ideas might seem a bit bizarre at first glance, believe it or not, the basic insight of Plato and Vedanta—that things aren't precisely what they appear to be and that underlying the perceived multiplicity in the universe is a far greater unity than we can possibly imagine—is actually being demonstrated by contemporary scientists in the field of quantum physics. The basic realization of quantum physics has be neatly summed up by American physicist, Barbara Brennan, in her book *The Hands of Light*:

> Through experiments over the past few decades physicists have discovered matter to be completely mutable into other particles or energy and vice-versa and on a subatomic level, matter does not exist with certainty in definite places, but rather shows 'tendencies' to exist. Quantum physics is beginning to realize that the Universe appears to be a dynamic web of interconnected and inseparable energy patterns. If the universe is indeed composed of such a web, there is logically no such thing as a part. This implies we are not separate parts of a whole but rather we are the Whole (24).

Sounds a bit familiar, doesn't it?

For centuries physicists, following Isaac Newton's lead, believed that the universe was composed of atoms that were solid in nature and attracted to each other by the force of gravity. What Albert Einstein discovered in the 20th century, however, was that atoms, and everything they joined together to form, consisted of subatomic particles that at their core were comprised of pure energy. Everything in the universe, in other worlds, at its core is made of the same basic stuff—energy. To use more metaphorical language, we exist in an infinite field of quantum energy in way similar that a drop of water exists in the ocean. But just as it is impossible to separate one drop of water in the ocean from another, so all things in the universe, although appearing distinct and separate to us, are in fact ALL ONE. What is amazing is how the science of quantum physics is substantiating the insights of many of the great religious traditions of the world—namely, that underlying what we perceive to be multiplicity is nothing other than total unity!

You Ain't What You Appear to Be

What do all these crazy ideas have to do with the way you understand your own life? Surely, you are what you appear to be, aren't you? Human beings, after all, are essentially bipedal primates, members of the species *Homo sapiens*, but separated by other primates because our highly developed brains enable us to engage in useful things like abstract reasoning, language, planning for the future, and problem solving. In the end aren't we basically baboons with better cognitive capacities, and this enables us to do things that other primates can't do—like create complex social structures?

For many scientists, that's the end of the story about who we are as human beings. But we know that there's more to us than just that. We are also artists, poets, philosophers, explorers of the unknown; we envision possibilities that don't even exists and turn them into reality; we have souls that are filled with some of the most sublime ideas ever imagined and thoughts so creepy and destructive that they are almost demonic.

But that's still only scratching the surface of who we are.

Let's assume for a moment that the basic insights of Plato, ancient Hinduism and Quantum Physics are correct and things truly aren't quite as they appear to be. This would imply that you yourself aren't quite what you appear to be either. So who are you then? We've spent 15 weeks asking this very question, so by now you should have some ideas, shouldn't you? Let's try it again…

Who Am I?

•

-
-
-
-
-

When I asked you the question, "Who Are You?" at the beginning of this program, you probably identified yourself, as most people do, with the basic aspects of the persona—appearance, personality, and beliefs. Or perhaps you focused on yourself as the protagonist in your own life story and would have identified yourself according to major events in your life or the other characters with whom you have interacted most intimately— family members, friends, and lovers. As you explored your wounded child, your shadow, and your fantastic self, you may have begun to see that there is definitely much more to who you are than meets the eye. And certainly on one level all that is the real you.

But on a deeper level, everything related to your personal identity is Maya—the great illusion of separateness and multiplicity that consciousness creates and which keeps us from recognizing who we actually are. If we strip away all illusion and self-deception, we know that you are no-thing, no-one, no-self.

If the basic premise of quantum physics is true there is nothing that separates us from other beings and the world around us. We truly are one with everything in the universe. You, me, the tree, the car, the state of Kentucky…we are all part of the same cosmic energy or consciousness. The only thing that keeps you from recognizing your basic oneness with other human beings and the world around you is your own egoistic self-absorption (your fixation on "I," "me," and "mine"). If you could but cleanse your mind, as Huxley advised us to do (remember our last chapter?) "every thing would appear…as it is, infinite." So who we are in a very deep and spiritual sense is definitely not this particular person, living in this place and time, but a being that is intimately connected with Being itself.

But more than that, if the insights of the great religious traditions of the world are true, we are also one with the Infinite Consciousness that is the source of all Being. You are, in other words part of the reality that we call Brahman, Yahweh, Allah, Christ, and the Buddha. The divine reality flows in you and through you; you are one with it, whether you recognize that or not.

While this might seem like a heretical proposition, pantheism and panentheism are actually the basis of most of the great religious traditions of the world. The pantheist believes that God is one with the world; the panentheist believes that God's being penetrates every part of the world while also extending beyond it. Although there are serious differences between these two traditions, what they both share in common is the belief that at the core level of reality, the divine essence permeates all things, and this includes you. As Meister Eckhardt, a 13th century Christian mystic, once put it:

> God is closer to me than I am to myself: my being depends on God's being near me and present to me. So God is also in a stone or a log of wood, only they do not know it. If the wood knew God and realized how close God is to it as the highest angel does, it would be as blissful as the highest angel. And so a human is more blessed than a stone or a piece of wood because she or he is aware of God and knows how close God is. And I am the more blessed, the more I realize this, and I am the less blessed, the less I know this. I am not blessed because God is in me and is near me and because I possess Him, but because I am aware of how close God is to me, and that I know God (165-166).

So God exists in all things, but he exists so intimately in us that we human beings have the possibility to recognize the divine nature that is at the core of our essence. Alone among all other creatures in the world we have been given the ability to tap into our own divine spark and use it to transform our own lives and the world around us.

Becoming aware of your own inner-divinity shouldn't make you arrogant or self-absorbed. Quite the opposite, actually. Arrogance and self-absorption are signs of ego at work ("I," "me," and "mine" again). Recognizing the oneness of all reality and your connection to all things, should bring with it a sense of wonder, amazement, and humility. The idea that there is nothing basically separating any of us from each other or from the rest of the world should be a source of personal liberation from the petty, superficial, restricted view of life that most people possess.

This realization, if taken to heart, should also lead you to live a much more authentic existence than you probably are right now. There is no need to prove anything to yourself or to anyone else about how wonderful you are, because in your essence you are totally and completely perfect. You don't have to try to be good, because, in fact, you are goodness itself, and compassion and kindness and truth and love. All you have to do is to recognize your inner divinity and live accordingly.

And, although you have probably been struggling for the past 15 weeks to unleash your creative self, you don't have to struggle any longer. You don't just simply possess a spark of creative energy, you are one with the ultimately source of all creativity. So when you create anything—a poem, a painting, a photo...anything at all—you are collaborating with that dynamic and infinite energy that created all things.

For Reflection

We've come a long way in this program, haven't we? From looking at your face in the mirror and thinking that the image that reflects back at you is the real you, we've now come to the point where we may have begun to recognize that who we are is so incredibly amazing that words can barely describe the kind of wonderful being that you actually are in the core of your essence.

Most people simply can't wrap their minds around the transcendent dimension of their human identity. Even those who are more spiritually inclined might need an entire lifetime of reflection—and perhaps multiple lifetimes, if you buy into an Eastern way of looking at life—before they can accept their own divine natures.

To help you explore this dimension of your personality, try reflecting on the following questions:

1. Picture yourself free of all limitations and imperfections. Imagine yourself as being completely and totally perfect just the way you are. Now describe this perfect you.

2. With the idea of your own limitless perfection in mind, now explain what you think the *real* purpose of your life might be.

3. If you could accept the idea of yourself as being completely and totally perfect just the way you are, would this realization change the way you are currently living your life? If so, how?

Express Yourself

It's time to end our self-exploration on a very positive note. For all the following exercises, put aside thoughts of your own personal limitations and failings and allow your wonderful, luminescent, divine self to shine through. It's time now to sing unabashed songs of praise to yourself, so drop any sense of false modesty and sing out loudly!

This kind of writing is best done in a beautiful, cozy, or at least peaceful, environment. If the weather is warm enough, take some pen and paper with you to the beach or a nature preserve and allow yourself to feel at one with the universe and the creative energy within it.

15.1. Record an Idealized Version of Your Life. This exercise comes from Kathleen Adam's *Journey to the Self*: "Close your eyes and think about what it would be like if your job, relationship, children, or sex life were perfect. Then write about your inner journey (58).

15.2. Saintly Acts. Sometimes we're so down on ourselves that we don't remember the generous, kind, compassionate things we often do in life. Think about a time in your life when you helped someone in need with no thought to your own benefit or reward. This doesn't have to be a momentous act, just one in which you reached out to someone who was in pain or suffering and tried in some way to make his or life a bit easier. Now write about this experience and how it made you feel.

15.3. The Really, Really Big Questions. "Who am I? Why am I here? What is the purpose of my life?" Just try answering these questions. They're the ones that have perplexed philosophers for centuries.

If you'd like you can write this one as a dialogue between yourself and God on the Day of Judgment.

15.4. What is Your Big Picture? This one comes from Sandy Grayson's *Journalution*:

> Imagine that all the people and situations that have caused you grief in the past have been magically transformed and understood as life lessons. They no longer take energy from you each day. Your slate is clean and you are ready to make your contribution to the world. Take a deep breath. Create a vision of yourself that encompasses the greatest dream you can hold for your life. Imagine that nothing is off limits, and you are ready to live a

big life. What could this be? What is the whisper that gives you butterflies in your belly? Write it down. Exhale the fear and allow your vision to flow onto the page. You don't have to worry about how to accomplish it right now; you must only capture the dream on the page. If you have several outrageous visions, write them all down (105).

15.5. Song of Myself. Write a poem or a song in praise of yourself, along the lines of Walt Whitman's "Song of Myself." Don't be afraid to go overboard in singing your own praises. Remember, you are marvelous!

15.6. Eulogy/Last Will and Testament. Pretend that you've just died and write a *eulogy* to yourself describing your accomplishments as a human being. A eulogy is all about praising a person's life, so don't hold back. Really, really praise yourself.

If writing a eulogy seems a bit egotistical to you, write a last will and testament. Pretend that you have just discovered that you have some kind of terminal illness and will be dead within a week. Then simply write down what you would say to the loved ones in your life.

15.7. Prayer of Thanksgiving. Write a prayer of gratitude for all the wonderful things in life. If you are having trouble thinking of many, then you are not being objective. No matter how difficult it might be, everyone's life is filled with at least some things or people for which to be grateful. If you've ever suffered though a life-threatening illness—or know someone who has—then you should realize that simply waking up every morning to a new day is cause for gratitude.

Start by listing ten things at this moment for which you are grateful. Then focus in on one of these and go into detail about why you are so appreciative for having it in your life.

15.8. Unsent Letter of Forgiveness. In a previous exercise, you were allowed to express you honest feelings about a person who may have wronged or harmed you in some way. In this letter, the focus is on healing and reconciliation. Write a letter to the person who hurt you, expressing your forgiveness for what they did to you. Although you might think that the person to whom you are writing the letter is not deserving of any forgiveness, the real point of this exercise, as Sandy Grason reminds us, is to free yourself from the crippling effects of hatred:

> Forgiveness is not something you do for another person. You do it for yourself to free yourself. Although you may not believe it's

working at the moment when you're doing it, each time you write the words "I forgive you for...[fill in the blank]" on the page, your heart will get a little lighter and your pent-up emotions will begin to evaporate. Once you begin to forgive, or at least to reach a state of acceptance about the past, you will attract the good things you want in life and start living more peacefully and joyfully today....I encourage you to practice forgiveness in your [writing] to release yourself. It takes a tremendous amount of energy to carry around anger, hatred, disappointment, frustration, and sadness. Everywhere you go, you carry these emotions, holding them inside your body. Forgiveness allows you to release the heavy, negative energy and move into a new day feeling lighter and more focused. Eventually the old emotions will no longer cloud your vision. You will be free to move past them and become who you truly are (62-63).

15.9. A Spiritual Moment. Describe a time in your life when you were totally happy and at peace with the world. Describe the experience in either prose or poetry.

If you prefer, you can try this exercise from Sandy Grason's *Journalution*:

Write about a time in your life when you felt particularly close to a higher power. If you are comfortable using the word "God" write about that. Otherwise you may think of Mother Earth or the energy that unites every living thing in the universe or whatever works for you. Write about how that connection felt: Did you feel guided in a certain direction? How did you feel physically? Did you feel energy coursing through your body? Did you hear a voice or whisper? What did it sound like? What was the experience like for you? Imagine that you are back in that moment right now. Feel it, breathe in the experience. Describe what was happening for you in as much detail as possible. Then see if you can re-create the experience right now in your [writing] (152).

15.10. Spiritual Guide Dialogue. Write a dialogue between yourself and your Spiritual Guide (e.g., God, Buddha, Jesus, your Higher Power, your guardian angel, or your divine Self). You can imagine yourself sitting on a beach or by a lake and then your spiritual guide comes by and sits down with you. At that point, you can ask your Spiritual Guide any question you'd like and rest assured that it will be answered with complete and total honesty.

Another possibility is to write a letter to or from your higher power (Adams, 179).

15.11. The Purpose of My Life. Do you believe that your life as a specific purpose or destiny? If so, write about it.

15.12. If Heaven Exists. Describe what you think heaven would be like if it does exist. You can write this in either prose or poetry. Or, if you prefer, imagine yourself dying and ascending up to heaven. Create an imaginary account of your experience moving into the next life as a dramatic scene or a piece of flash fiction.

Appendices

Some Practical Tips for Creative Expression

Appendix A
Beginning to Write

Although there are no rules in the Creative Self program, here are a few suggestions that might help you in getting started with your writing. After you read over these suggestions, feel free to adapt them or discard them as you see fit:

Forget About Quality (At First)

It doesn't matter whether what you write is boring, confusing, or even only semiliterate. Turn off the inner censor and just start writing. Later in the program, you will have ample opportunity to "fix up" what you have written. For now, all we expect you to do is get some words onto paper. You should also not try to worry very much if you are writing in "correct" English or in a sophisticated enough style. Unless you have specific reasons for doing otherwise, you can feel free to use vernacular language—to write, in other words, the way that you typically speak—or even to make up your own language and syntax. Focus more on self-expression and worry about correctness some other time.

Be Personal

We know that for most of your education your English teachers have advised you to avoid using the world "I" and try to keep your writing as objective as possible. But in this program, "I," "me," and "mine" are the most important words that you will ever use. As Sheila Bender says, "Just as you dream your own dreams, you live your own experiences. You are the filter for what you see, hear, taste, touch and smell in the world....You must own your experience, every detail of it, to write well about it." (7).

Write from your personal experience and use the word "I" as often as you need to fully capture your own unique perspective as a human being.

In the kind of writing that we are doing in this program, you can't possibly be too self-focused or too self-absorbed. When writing about any event in your life, then, the most things to ask yourself are: (1) How do I feel or what do I think about this situation? (2) What was my response or reaction to the situation? (3) What did I leave unsaid or undone? (4) What did I learn as a result of this situation?

Be as Honest as You Can (Or Are Willing to Be)

There is always a certain amount of trepidation involved in attempting to write about your inner thoughts and intimate feelings. It is important, however, that you avoid attempting to write about what you think will be acceptable to others and just be as honest as you can about who you are. Honesty in writing, as Tristine Rainer, observes, " has less to do with the 'truth' than the way you reveal your 'real self' as distinguished from the social roles you play and masks you wear to make an impression. It involves an openness about what you really feel, what you want, what you really believe, what you really decide" (35). It is your job in writing to unveil the authentic YOU, whoever that might be and regardless of how acceptable it may be to others. As Sandy Grason notes, this sort of openness involves a great deal of courage on the part of a writer:

> Your goal is to discover your beliefs, no matter what others may think. Trust your inner wisdom, follow your intuition, and listen to your heart. Write the longings of your soul, and be willing to go out on a limb to express yourself. Your true voice will show up, and if you let it sing to you, it will get stronger and stronger. It all starts with a willingness to write down anything that comes into your mind (29).

It is completely up to you to determine with whom you will share your writing. As you get more comfortable sharing intimate thoughts and feelings with others, you will probably find the process liberating. And who knows, you may just come to enjoy becoming a literary exhibitionist!

Make Use of Vivid Details and Descriptions

In order to effectively convey your experiences to others, it is important that you write with as much detail about these experiences as you possibly can. This means using language and images derived from all of your senses. Don't just talk about your grandmother's living room; tell your reader what sights, sounds, and smells you experience when you walk into it. The use of such sensory detail should "show" the reader what you are describing and make him feel as though he were present with you.

Select Words and Images Thoughtfully

Are you describing a large man or a gargantuan walrus of a man? Does the meal you are eating taste good or is it delectable? You are in command of the words and images you use in your writing, so choose them consciously to convey exactly what you want to convey. This is the reason that really wonderful writers always have thesauruses at arm's length when they are writing anything (even a postcard!).

It's Ok to Steal

All great writers borrow from other great writers. That's how they learn to develop their own style. During the course of this program, you will be exposed to many different styles of writing. Feel free to steal ideas from any of the writers you encounter in this text (or anywhere else for that matter). The only caveat is that, if you choose to model a piece you write on the style of someone else, you try to put your own unique spin on what you write, so that it is truly your own. You might also give credit to your source by putting something like "after [Author's Name]" below your own title.

Get Feedback Often

If your creative work is to improve over time, it is extremely important to receive on-going constructive criticism. While such criticism should always be kind in tone, it should also be concrete enough to actually help you improve your writing. This is also true when you are taking on the role of a critic: when you are responding to what others have written, it's not enough simply to write, "great work" or "I really loved this piece." Be specific about what you thought was terrific about the writing and what could be improved. And be prepared to have others do the same for your own work.

In the end, revisit and rewrite. Only much later in this program will we encourage you to revisit what you have previously written with an eye to improving your writing. But, when we get to that point, it will be extremely important that you take the time to rework every decent piece that you have written with the aim of making it truly outstanding. When you get around to reworking your writing, you might also consider having someone with a fairly decent command of the English language look over your work, correct any grammatical or spelling mistakes that were not intentional, and give you some recommendations on how to improve specific pieces of writing.

Appendix B
Unleashing Your Inner Poet

It may seem strange, but many people are terrified at the thought of writing poetry: some are afraid that what they write will sound silly or preposterous; others that their own poetry could never measure up to the kinds of poems that they read in high school English class; and still others that people will think they are effete or pretentious for even daring to write poetry. Because of these sorts of fears, the vast majority of people on the planet probably never even attempt to write a poem unless they are forced to in school.

While some people have fairly grandiose ideas about what poetry is all about, we take a much simpler approach. Poetry is nothing more than an attempt to convey powerful impressions or feelings in a direct, concise, and aesthetically engaging manner. We saw an example of this in Chapter One with Keisha's coneflower poem. The poem takes all of Keisha's conflicted feelings about her father's coneflowers and expresses them in poetic form.

Although we hesitate to burden you with rules to follow when writing poetry, a few gentle guidelines might be helpful if you've never written poetry before:

1. Poetry always begins from personal experience.

Don't try to write a poem based upon someone else's experience or about something that isn't extremely important to you. You can only write about subjects you know, and you can only write well about subjects you know well. This is true for good prose writing as well, but it is even more applicable to poetry, which is the most personal form of writing imaginable. So, avoid writing epic poems about medieval knights in the 11th century and stick to you own perfectly fascinating life experiences (unless you were an 11th century knight in a previous life and are having some very powerful flashbacks!).

2. Focus on experiences that generate powerful emotions.

You certainly could write a poem about something mundane (taking out the garbage, waiting for the bus), but unless you feel passionately—or at least somewhat strongly—about these subjects, you'll have a difficult time writing a poem about them. Here's something for you to think about: What experience have you had recently that generated a deep emotional reaction within you? Perhaps you were slighted recently and are feeling angry about it or maybe you met someone special who caused romantic (or sexual) feelings to rise up inside you or perhaps you were sitting in a park and felt an overflowing sense of inner peace. Those kinds of powerful experiences are the place to start when thinking about poems to write.

3. Describe the experience and the emotions they generated.

Don't describe it poetically yet. Just get your ideas down on paper in straightforward prose or stream-of-consciousness writing. When he was thinking what to write a poem about, Cory Stumlauter, a novice poet, immediately thought of the strong feelings of resentment that he had because of all the expectations placed upon him by his family and the people at work. He began with a stream-of-consciousness rant:

> Everyone expects me to be happy all the time, and cheerfully greet them with a big-ole smile to help make everything run smoothly. They all want me to grovel and serve them, to bow my head like some kind of damned serf…. to be silent and anonymous and to remain totally invisible. But I'm not gonna do that today, no way. Today is my day, damn it! A time for me to turn totally inward and take care of myself for a change. And everyone around me, everyone who wants a little something more from me, they are just interlopers in the endless fantasies running through my mind. Today I just want to be left alone; tomorrow I'll take care of all the stupid obligations that I have and play the serf again with that big-ole smile once again on my face. But just not today.

4. Translate your thoughts into poetic form.

Once you have some ideas written down, the next step is to arrange the lines into interesting poetic form. How you do this exactly is your own call, but generally will involve playing around with line breaks and adjusting the words and images you use. Here's Cory's attempt at a first stanza of poetry based upon what he had previously written.

They may expect me to smile politely
And greet them cheerfully with a big-ole smile
To help smooth out your social intercourse.
But I'm not gonna do that, today.
No way!

5. Rework what you have written.

Despite what some writers have said, your first thought is usually not your best thought, and even the greatest poets have worked and reworked lines of poetry to make them flow more smoothly. Looking at his first stanza, Cory realizes that he could do better in expressing his feelings poetically. Here's the modified version he finally came up with:

I may smile politely
and nod my head with cheerful greetings
to help grease the rusty wheels of
social intercourse...
But not today.

Notice that the sentiment that Cory expresses is basically the same as in his first attempt—his frustration at being put upon by others. The major difference is that he has tightened up his language and has worked to make the poem flow a bit more smoothly. He also has a final line for the stanza that can serve as a kind of refrain. Once his first stanza was polished some more, the next two came out fairly rapidly

I may smile politely
and nod my head with heartfelt greetings
and obsequious platitudes
to help grease the rusty wheels of
social intercourse...
But not today.

I may grovel and serve
and grant the right of way
to all of you who delight
in calling yourselves my masters
But not today.

I may shuffle along the busy track
an invisible member of the anonymous pack

content only to go unnoticed
in a sea of harried faces...
But not today.

6. Rework some more.

As the lines of your poem flow onto paper, begin to examine your word
choices, aiming at economy of expression. Try to use language that
vividly reveals the images and sentiments you want to convey to your
reader. When examining what you have written, ask, Is this precisely what
I am trying to achieve with this word, this image, this line, this stanza?
Focusing on his second two stanzas, Cory realized that they could be
improved with slightly different word choices:

> I may bow and serve
> and grant the right of way
> time and again
> to you and your uptown kind...
> But not today.

> I may shuffle along the cityscape
> an invisible member of the anonymous pack
> content only to go unnoticed
> in a sea of harried humanity...
> But not today.

After writing the first three stanzas, the rest of the poem came quite easily
to Cory. After about five more revisions, he was ready to submit his work.
The finished product actually turned out to be quite a wonderful reflection
of his feelings at the time he wrote the poem:

But Not Today

> I may smile politely
> and nod my head with heartfelt greetings
> and obsequious platitudes
> to help grease the rusty wheels of
> social intercourse...
> But not today.

> I may grovel and serve
> and grant the right of way

time and again
to you and your uptown kind...
But not today.

I may shuffle along the cityscape
an invisible member of the anonymous pack
content only to go unnoticed
in a sea of harried humanity...
But not today.

Today is for me and mine,
not for you and yours,
a day for glorious self-absorption
and cosmic autofixated revelries,
in which I am
the Supreme Unmoved-Mover
in my own self-contained universe.
Today is my day
and mine alone,
and you, dear friend,
are the uninvited interloper
in the myopic monologues
and solipsistic soliloquies
running through the endless channels
of my own egocentric mindspace.

Tomorrow there will be time again
for duties and obligations,
for oughts and musts and have-tos,
for all the silly stupid demands
the others so capriciously
seek to impose.
Tomorrow I will play
the serf yet again
and graciously do
my masters' biddings
with winsome charm
and gentle subservience...

But not today.

If you think you can't write a poem, think again. The first thing you need to do, though, is get over your precomceived notions of what poetry is or should be. You don't have to write like Shakespeare to be an effective poet. All you have to do is be willing to tap into your own inner resources and honestly express what you are feeling.

The rest of poetry writing is simply a matter of polishing and refining. If you simpy express your feeling honestly on paper, you'll probably write a decent poem. But if you are willing to take the time to consider your word choices, imagery, and the overall structure of your poem, you'll have the possbility to create something truly amazing.

Appendix C
Flash Story Telling

There is one form of writing that lends itself most appropriately to recounting significant events from the past—story telling. The great events of your life are automatically the stuff of stories, since they have a certain amount of drama necessarily built into them. If the prospect of having to write a full-blown short story with complicated plot devices frightens the hell out of you, put your mind at ease. The kind of story-telling that we are going to encourage you to do is so easy that just about anyone can do it in the same amount of time that it would take to write a standard journal entry.

Let's start by understanding what we actually mean by the word "story." A story, writes Roberta Allen in *Fast Fiction,* is simply

> a container in which something happens. That something needs to create an experience for the reader....The story can be an incident, an episode, an anecdote, a fable, a parable, a fantasy, a monologue, or a fiction disguised as an essay. A story can simply present a change in a character's state of mind or point of view. The change may be a realization, a revelation, an epiphany, an understanding, or a decision. It might result in finding a lost dog, nursing a sick man back to health, falling in love for the first time, or deciding to sell a house.

Every decent story, no matter how long or short it is, has certain common elements: well developed, interesting characters, a distinct time or setting, a particular point of view (either first or third person), and coherent and engaging plot structure with a clear point (Allen, 39-46).

Short stories, whether fiction or non-fiction, can vary in length from a paragraph to several thousand words. Having been used to reading longer, more complex short stories by writers such as Hemingway and Faulkner in school, many first time writers are intimidated by the prospect of writing stories. For this program, however, we specifically encourage you to think small. During the past ten years a new type of story was developed that is referred to as "sudden fiction," "flash fiction" or "short shorts." Whether they are recounting true life or fictitious events, what all these stories have in common is that they are super brief: normally between 500 and 1000 words…or less than one page typewritten. They also have a beginning, a middle, and end just like any other story.

If you think it's easy to tell a story in under 1000 words, just try it some time. For a start, use interesting events from your own life that can be told in story form. Here's one person's account about a seemingly trivial incident from his childhood that made a much larger impact on him than one would expect:

The Wrong Joe
By A.J. Grunthaler

My 7th birthday. Today was going to be my day to stick it to the jerks on the block. It was the days of the G.I. Joe craze, when every self-respecting lad of 7 or 8 had at least two or three Joes and a slew of necessary accessories (various weapons, uniforms, jeeps, and the like).

Now there was a definite hierarchy among the Joes and everyone, no matter how limited they were intellectually, understood this hierarchy intuitively and respected it: The standard regulation Joe with the black beard was either a private or a corporal; the African American Joe—which, for some reason, none of the Italian or Irish kids in the neighborhood seemed to have—was a sergeant; the non-bearded Joe was a lieutenant or captain; and the gray haired Joe was a colonel. The ranks for each Joe also depended upon your place in the complex hierarchy of the block and varied depending upon how old or how tough you were.

Today, for once, was going to be my day. Today was the first day that Hasbro, the maker of the G.I. Joe action figures (Don't even think about calling them dolls!) was coming out with the white haired Joe, who we had all already determined had to be the general. In an act of uncharacteristic compassion, my mother had agreed that, while she was shopping on Roosevelt Ave., she would stop into Toy City and buy me the white haired Joe for my birthday. I would be the first kid on the block to have him and, therefore, because of the rules of seniority, would always have the highest-ranking G.I. Joe on the block.

I tried to be cool about the whole thing, but I know that I

probably couldn't help rubbing my good fortune into the faces of my less than delighted pals. We were playing on the street, when in the distance I could see my mother's hobbit-like frame waddle down the street pushing a shopping cart. "This is it," I shouted as loudly as I could to all my friends. "This is the moment when I get to be the one in charge, the guy givin' the orders." My friends gritted their teeth and I could hear them cursing under their breaths. But what could they do? The rules were the rules.

I ran down the street as fast as I could. My mother had the usual look of apathy on her face, but perhaps because it was my birthday she didn't greet me with her usual, "Will you just leave me the hell alone until I get inside." Instead she put her hand into the cart and slowly lifted out the large bag she had inside. It had the famous "Toy City" logo on it, so I knew that my wildest dreams were about to come true.

"Here's your damn toy," my mother said, dropping the package in my hands. "Now go play with your friends and try not to bother me for a few hours, will you?"

I ran as fast as I could with the package to the spot where my friends were playing. They were all looking up at me with incredible envy in their eyes.

"Well here he is," I said, proudly pulling Joe out of his brown paper wrapping. "Get ready to start taking commands."

I pulled Joe out of the bag and lifted him up like the sacred object that he was and waited for the oooohs and ahhhhhs of admiration from my friends.

"Look at that!" I heard fat Ricky shout out. "Your mother really screwed you over this time." In seconds, everyone was joining him laughing at me.

I turned the box around and gasped in horror. Instead of the white haired Joe, who would be giving commands forever, my mother in her usual state of confusion had accidentally bought the red haired Joe—the one we had determined was the doctor, the one who couldn't give any commands at all, the one, in short, who no one in his right mind would ever want to have. The poor bastard wasn't even able to fight. All he could do was hang around in the "hospital," waiting until someone came in with an injury. And the reality was that no one's Joe in the entire history of the G.I. Joe Universe ever got injured. They might get their head or limbs ripped off, but they never would waste their time going to see some candy-ass red haired Joe doctor.

"Hey, A.J.," Rudy said. "I got a mole on my ass. Do you

think your Dr. Joe could check it out for me? He, he, he…"

"What an idiot!" I heard someone say as I walked back home, my head hung in abject shame.

"How did the boys like your new doll?" my mother asked as she stirred the sausage and peppers she was making for dinner.

"It's not a doll," I snapped. "And you got the wrong one. I asked you to get me the doll—I mean action figure—with the white hair. You got me the one with the red hair."

"White, red…What's the difference?" my mother said oblivious to my agony. "They're all the same anyway. Just pretend you have the white haired one."

Just pretend I had the white haired one. If only I could have pretended that my entire existence up until that point was just a cruel nightmare that I would one day wake up from, then I might have some consolation. Right now, though, it was just me and the doc—two sad, pathetic losers who were victims of a chronically unjust, consistently absurd universe.

And these were supposed to be the good years.

The author of this story admits that he magnified the events described and his reactions so that his story would be more interesting to the reader and that he also portrayed his mother as being much harsher than she actually was in real life. How precisely he recounts this event from the past, however, is really not important. What is important is that the author was able to go back into his past, dreg up a significant event from his life, tell the story that is complete and fairly humorous, and at the same time give the reader a glimpse into his personal life at the time.

When using flash storytelling to write about real life incidents, you can embellish or exaggerate the drama of the incidents you describe—just make sure that what you recount is grounded in something that actually happened to you. Later on, after you've developed the knack of telling stories from your own life, you can try your hand at fiction and fantasy story telling.

Tips for Flash Story Telling

As you write your flash pieces there are a few things to remember:

1. *Short doesn't mean boring.* Although your flash pieces should be short, you shouldn't skimp on the descriptive elements that make for a good story. Do you have well-defined characters, an interesting plot, and a clear setting for your tale? If any of these pieces are missing, then your story will necessarily suffer.

2. Plot the plot before you write it. A good story plot always includes development, a conflict, and some kind of resolution. Think through these elements before you begin to write or your story will probably ramble about incoherently and bore your reader.

3. Don't forget to include dialogue. Sometimes a story can simply be told as a conversation between two or more characters without much description at all. In this case the conversation itself develops the plot and fleshes out the characters in your story. But good dialogue doesn't come cheaply. It takes work to capture the essence of a character in a short piece of writing through the few lines of dialogue that you have to work with.

4. Feel free to go gonzo. When you're writing about the great stories of your life, you need not scrupulously adhere to the literal truth about the events you are recording. If it makes things more interesting for you, try going a bit gonzo in your story-telling. The term "Gonzo Journalism" was made popular by Hunter S. Thompson in the early 1970s and refers to writing that is neither strict objective reporting nor complete fiction, but a hybrid of the two. In many of his works Thompson completely abandons the pretense of objectivity to get to the truth of the subject about which he is writing. Outright lying, gross exaggeration, and distortions of reality are all perfectly acceptable in gonzo writing as long as they get to the deeper—i.e., subjective—truth of the experience being reported upon.

Appendix D
Self-Publishing

The goal of creative expression is not simply to create works of art solely for yourself, but to share the fruits of your labor with others. In the not-too-distant past, only a small number of writers and artists ever got to see their work published and shared with a wider audience. The advent of digital publishing, however, has changed all that. Now with programs like Blurb (www.blurb.com), Lulu (www.lulu.com), and Createspace (www.createspace.com) you can create your own unique work and make it available to whomever you want for a fairly reasonable price. These programs are all POD (publishing on demand) programs, which means you only have to pay for the number of copies you want for yourself and your friends.

If you really feel ambitious you can even take the work that you create and self-publish it on the Internet for a wider reading audience. The programs that I've mentioned above will actually enable you to produce a bookstore quality work that most people probably wouldn't even realize is self-published unless you told them. If you feel confident about the quality of your work, you can then "publish" it on Amazon.com and avoid having to deal with publishing companies at all. In fact, many authors who were published in the past by large publishing companies are now deciding to go the self-publishing route because it enables them to maintain more control over what they create and keep more of the royalties for themselves.

But even if you share the work that you create with no one else, there's something quite special about putting together your own book—whether it's simply a volume of your poems, a random collection of your thoughts, or a fully realized novel. For one thing, there's a sense of immense satisfaction that people get when they see their writing put together in book form. I've actually had students tell me that they almost cried when they saw their finished product. Your completed book will also become a keepsake that you can refer back to later on in life and a family heirloom that you can pass on to future generations.

If you've been faithfully following this program for the past 15 weeks, by now you probably have pages of material that you've written that can be put together in book form. There are several steps that usually need to be followed in order to get your text ready for self-publishing.

1. Continue Polishing What You've Written

There are some writers who are able to realize their creative visions in a single draft, but these are exceptions to the rule of publishing. In getting your own writing ready for self-publishing, the first thing you need to do is go back and polish what you've written. Then go back and polish it some more.

How many times should you go back and rework what you've written? A friend of mine who recently had a work of his successfully published told me that he rewrote each passage of his text about 50 times. In fact, he knew the text so well after reworking so much that he could recite what he had written to me without looking at the pages. This may not seem like such an impressive feat if one is producing a small collection of poems, but he was writing a work of history that was over a 1000 pages long!

No one expects you to rework what you have written quite as much as this, but make no mistake about it: writing for publication is an extremely labor intensive activity. If you are not willing to work extremely hard to perfect your writing, then simply publish for yourself and leave it at that.

2. Develop a Logical Plan for Your Work

If you have poems or stories that you want to put together into book form, you need to think through how you are going to organize what you've written. Of course, you can simply randomly place pieces of writing, but your overall work won't have the same impact as if it were more coherently organized. Think about arranging your writing topically and using subdivisions to separate your work into different sections.

In a typical text, the first page that you will see reproduces the cover information and normally includes the title and author of the text. On the opposite side of the inner cover page you will usually find copywrite information and on the page opposite that, the book's table of contents. I'd recommend looking at a number of books to get ideas for the design of your own work.

As you lay out your text, keep in mind that you should be thinking in terms of two page spreads, with even pages on the left and odd pages on the right. This is especially important to remember if your work has a number of shorter pieces or you want to include art or photography.

3. Think About a Catchy Title

A good title should do two things: it should be interesting enough that it should make someone want to actually read what you've written and it should accurately reflect what your work is about. It pays to take time to think through your title...even to agonize over it.

4. Lay Out Your Work

Programs like Createspace require self-publishers to know a little bit about layout and design issues. At the very least, if you use a program like this one, you will need to be able to create a pdf file for your completed text that meets Createspace's publishing requirements. To really make the most of this program, you need to be familiar with desktop publishing software like In Design, which is expensive to buy and somewhat difficult to use.

For most people interested in self-publishing, a far more practical option is use on-line programs like Blurb or Lulu, which provide templates that make laying out a text and creating attractive covers a snap. Of course, you are somewhat limited in design options when you use a program like Blurb or Lulu, but these programs do take some of the chore out of layout and design.

5. Design Your Cover

Like your title, the cover of your text is one of the first things anyone will notice about your work, so it pays to the time to design it properly. All of the programs I've metioned provide fairly easy to use cover templeates, so even if you know nothing about cover design, you should be able to create an attactive cover without much difficulty at all. Just take the time to think through what you want your front and back covers to say and what elements you will include on them.

6. Publish Your Book

Once you have your text and cover laid out and have carefully proofed your whole project, it's time to order your copy of the text. This is the most exciting part of the publishing process for a would-be author. If you use a POD type publishing program, you only need to order one book at a time. And it's a very good idea to order one copy as a proof to look over before you decide to order more for family and friends. You'd be absolutely amazed at how many errors you are likley to catch once you have a hard copy in your hands.

If you are completely happy with the way your work came out, then you have several options: If you think that it's really well done, you can try to sell it on Amazon.com. If it's a masterpiece, you can send copies to publishing companies that specialize in books like yours. Just make sure that your work really is a masterpiece though: rejection is part and parcel of the publishing process, and most would-be authors must have tremendous perseverence in order to succeed.

Of course, even if you produce one copy of a finished work just for yourself, you should consider yourself an enormous success. Most people never even complete a sustained creative work, let alone bother to go through the process of self-publishing their works.

If you've gotten that far, you should feel an emormous sense of self-complishment. Congratulations!

Sources

Adams, Kathleen. *Journal to the Self*. New York: Warner Books, 1990.

Addonizio, Kim and Laux, Dorianne. *The Poet's Companion*. New York: W.W. Norton, 1997.

Allen, Roberta. *Fast Fiction: Creating Fiction in Five Minutes*. Cincinnati, OH: Story Press, 1997.

Arieti, Silviano. *Creativity: The Magic Synthesis*. New York: Basic Books, 1976.

Bender, Sheila. *A Year in the Life: Journaling for Self-Discovery*. Cincinnati, OH: Writer's Digest Books, 2000.

—. *Writing Personal Essays: How to Shape Your Life Experiences for the Page*. Cincinnati, OH: Writer's Digest Books, 1995.

Bradshaw, John. *Homecoming: Reclaiming and Championing Your Inner Child*. New York: Bantam, 1992.

Brennan, Barbara. *The Hands of Light*. New York: Bantam, 1988.

Cameron, Julia. *The Artist's Way*. New York: Penguin Putnam, 2002.

Csikszentmihalyi, Mihaly. *Creativity*. New York: HarperCollins, 1997.

—. *Flow: The Psychology of Optimal Experience*. New York: Harper and Row, 1991.

Dacey, John S. *Fundamentals of Creative Thinking*. Lexington, MA: Lexington Books, 1989.

deBono, Edward. *Lateral Thinking*. New York: Harper and Row, 1970.

Eckhart, Meister. *Sermons and Treatises*. Vol. 2. Trans. M. O'C Walshe. Longmead: Element Books, 1987.

Fox, John. *Poetic Medicine: The Healing Art of Poem-Making*. New York: Putnam, 1997.

Fromm, Erich. *The Art of Loving*. New York: Harper and Row, 1956.

Goldberg, Natalie. *Writing Down the Bones*. Boston: Shambhala, 2005.

Goldman, Alan H. "Plain Sex." *Philosophy and Public Affairs* 6 (Spring 1977): 267-281.

Grason, Sandy. *Journalution*. Novato, CA: New World Library, 2005.

Huxley, Aldous. *The Doors of Perception*. New York: Harper Brothers, 1954.

Johnson, Robert. *Owning Your Own Shadow: Understanding the Dark Side of the Psyche*. San Francisco: HarperSanFrancisco, 1993.

—. *Transformation: Understanding the Three Levels of Mascul.* New York: HarperCollins, 1989.

Jung, Carl. *Collected Works*. 20 Volumes. Trans. Gerhard Adler and R.F.C. Hull. Princeton: Princeton University Press: 1979.

Keisey, David. *Please Understand Me*. Del Mar, CA: Prometheus Nemesis Books, 1998.

Kneller, George. *The Art and Science of Creativity*. New York: Holt, Rinehart and Winston, 1965.

Kurpis, Edward. "Becoming an Imperfectionist" from *Inspiring Creativity*. Ed. Rick Benzel. Playa del Rey, CA: Creative Coaching Association, 2005.

Langer, Ellen J. *On Becoming an Artist*. New York: Ballentine, 2005.

Lewis, C.S. *The Four Loves*. New York: Harcourt Brace, 1988.

Loori, John Daido. *The Zen of Creativity*. New York: Ballantine Books, 2004.

Maisel. Eric. *Fearless Creating*. New York: Penguin Putnam, 1995.

May, Rollo. *Courage to Create*. New York: W.W. Norton, 1975.

Miller, William A. *Make Friends with Your Shadow*. Minneapolis: Auguburg, 1981.

Nelson, G. Lynn. *Writing and Being: Taking Back Our Lives Through the Power of Language*. San Diego, CA: LuraMedia, 1994.

Piirto, Jane. *Understanding Creativity*. Scottsdale, AR: Great Potential Press, 2004.

Progoff, Ira. *At a Journal Workshop*. New York: G.P. Putnam's Sons, 1992.

Rainer, Tristine. *The New Diary*. New York: St. Martin's Press, 1978.

Rimbaud, Arthur. *Complete Poetry and Prose*. New York: Modern Library, 2003.

Rogers, Carl R. "Towards a Theory of Creativity." *ETC: A Review of General Semantics* 11 (1954): 249-260.

Storer, Dave. "Creativity is Your Birthright." *Inspiring Creativity*. Ed. Rick Benzel. Playa del Rey, CA: Creative Coaching Association, 2005.

Suzuki, Shunryu. *Zen Mind, Beginner's Mind*. Boston: Weatherhill, 1970.

Thompson, Chic. *What a Great Idea 2.0*. New York: Sterling, 2007.

Zinn, Jon Kabat-Zinn. *Full Catastrophe Living*. New York: Random House, 1990.

Photo Credits

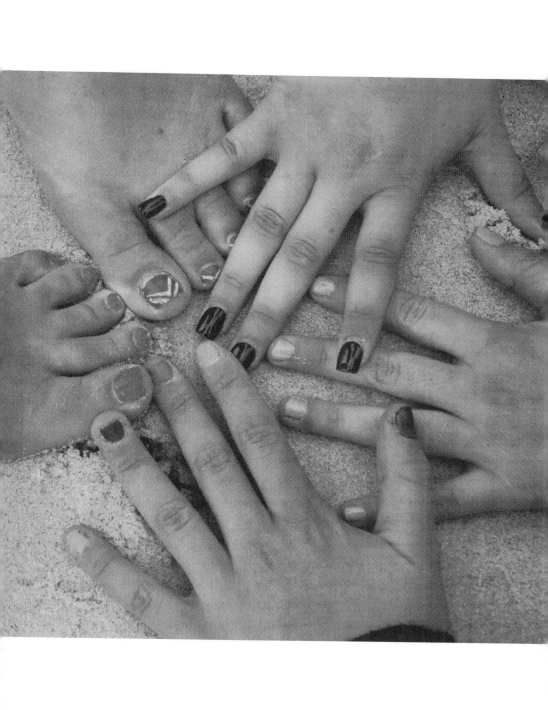

Made in the USA
Charleston, SC
15 December 2013